Family, Unvalued

Discrimination, Denial, and the Fate of Binational Same-Sex Couples under U.S. Law

HUMAN RIGHTS WATCH

IMMIGRATION EQUALITY

Printed in the United States of America ISBN: 1-56432-336-6
Cover photos: © 2006 Private Cover design by Rafael Jimenez

Immigration Equality
350 West 31st Street, Suite 505
New York, NY 10001
Tel. +1 (212) 714-2904
Fax +1 (212) 714-2973
E-mail: info@immigrationequality.org
www.immigrationequality.org

Human Rights Watch
350 Fifth Avenue, 34th floor
New York, NY 10118-3299 USA
Tel: 1-(212) 290-4700, Fax: 1-(212) 736-1300
hrwnyc@hrw.org

1630 Connecticut Avenue, N.W., Suite 500
Washington, DC 20009 USA
Tel:1-(202) 612-4321, Fax:1-(202) 612-4333
hrwdc@hrw.org

2nd Floor, 2-12 Pentonville Road
London N1 9HF, UK
Tel: 44 20 7713 1995, Fax: 44 20 7713 1800
hrwuk@hrw.org

Rue Van Campenhout 15,
1000 Brussels, Belgium
Tel: 32 (2) 732-2009, Fax: 32 (2) 732-0471
hrwatcheu@skynet.be

9 rue Cornavin
1201 Geneva, Switzerland
Tel: +41 22 738 04 81, Fax: +41 22 738 17 91
hrwgva@hrw.org

Poststraße 4-5
10178 Berlin, Germany
Tel. +49 30 259 306 10, Fax. +49 30 259 306 29
berlin@hrw.org

Web Site Address: http://www.hrw.org

HUMAN RIGHTS WATCH

Human Rights Watch is dedicated to protecting the human rights of people around the world.

We stand with victims and activists to prevent discrimination, to uphold political freedom, to protect people from inhumane conduct in wartime, and to bring offenders to justice.

We investigate and expose human rights violations and hold abusers accountable.

We challenge governments and those who hold power to end abusive practices and respect international human rights law.

We enlist the public and the international community to support the cause of human rights for all.

IMMIGRATION EQUALITY

Immigration Equality is a national organization that works to end immigration discrimination against lesbian, gay, bisexual, transgender, and HIV-positive people.

Immigration Equality provides legal services, information, and support to immigrants, activists, attorneys, and legislators.

We help win asylum in the United States for those persecuted in their home country because of their sexual orientation, transgender identity, or HIV-status.

Through education, outreach, advocacy, and the maintenance of a nationwide network of resources, we fight for those who are threatened by persecution or the discriminatory impact of immigration law.

Human Rights Watch conducts regular, systematic investigations of human rights abuses in some seventy countries around the world. Our reputation for timely, reliable disclosures has made us an essential source of information for those concerned with human rights. We address the human rights practices of governments of all political stripes, of all geopolitical alignments, and of all ethnic and religious persuasions. Human Rights Watch defends freedom of thought and expression, due process and equal protection of the law, and a vigorous civil society; we document and denounce murders, disappearances, torture, arbitrary imprisonment, discrimination, and other abuses of internationally recognized human rights. Our goal is to hold governments accountable if they transgress the rights of their people.

Human Rights Watch began in 1978 with the founding of its Europe and Central Asia division (then known as Helsinki Watch). Today, it also includes divisions covering Africa, the Americas, Asia, Europe and Central Asia and the Middle East and North Africa. In addition, it includes three thematic divisions on arms, children's rights, and women's rights. It maintains offices in Berlin, Brussels, Geneva, London, Los Angeles, Moscow, New York, San Francisco, Tashkent, Toronto, and Washington. Human Rights Watch is an independent, nongovernmental organization, supported by contributions from private individuals and foundations worldwide. It accepts no government funds, directly or indirectly.

Acknowledgements

This report was written by Scott Long, director of the Lesbian, Gay, Bisexual and Transgender (LGBT) Rights Program of Human Rights Watch; Jessica Stern, researcher in the LGBT Rights Program of Human Rights Watch; and Adam Francoeur, program coordinator of Immigration Equality. Jessica Stern conducted the bulk of the interviews with assistance from Adam Francoeur and Scott Long.

The report is based on research conducted between 2003 and 2006. Immigration Equality surveyed binational same-sex couples via questionnaire between March 2003 and November 2004; they received approximately 900 responses that laid the groundwork for future documentation and conceptual development. In late 2004, Human Rights Watch and Immigration Equality formally decided to collaborate on this report. Human Rights Watch and Immigration Equality conducted interviews via telephone and in-person around the United States between October 2004 and January 2006 with thirty-three binational same-sex couples. Sixteen were lesbian-identified, fifteen were gay-identified, and two had one partner who was transgender. In addition to the range of countries represented among the 900 survey respondents, the non-citizen partners among the couples interviewed were from: Argentina, Australia, the Bahamas, Belgium, Brazil, Canada, Colombia, Denmark, France, Germany, Italy, Jamaica, the Netherlands, Rwanda, Spain, Taiwan, Turkey, the United Kingdom, Uruguay, and Venezuela. Numerous people in the U.S. and in exile around the world who cannot be named for reasons of security participated in this research in invaluable ways. We give our deep thanks to the many couples and individuals we worked with on this report.

At Human Rights Watch, this report was edited by Joe Saunders, deputy program director; Dinah Pokempner, general counsel; Alison Parker, senior researcher in the U.S. Program; and Jamie Fellner, director of the U.S. Program. We are grateful to our colleagues for the advice they gave us: Rebecca Schleifer, researcher in the HIV/AIDS Program; Joe Amon, director of the HIV/AIDS Program; and William Frelick, director of Refugee Policy. Andrea Holley, manager of Outreach and Public Education, provided endless support with all aspects of production. We give our deep thanks to Jessica Robertson, intern in the LGBT Rights Program, who provided critical research assistance and beyond. Lance Lattig, media editor, provided communications advice. Liba Beyer, associate director, Development and Outreach, was instrumental in developing outreach and advocacy strategies.

Human Rights Watch expresses its gratitude to Henry van Ameringen, Alvin H. Baum, the David Bohnett Foundation, the David Geffen Foundation, the Gaylord and Dorothy Donnelley Foundation the Gill Foundation, James C. Hormel and Timothy

Wu, the Pomegranate Foundation, Ann B. Snitow, Jeanne and Joseph Sullivan, the Tides Foundation, and Reid Williams for their ongoing support of its work on lesbian, gay, bisexual and transgender people's rights.

Immigration Equality thanks its entire office along with former staff and interns. Specifically, we thank Lavi Soloway, Jennifer Higgins, Pradeep Singla, April Herms, and Heather Betz for their advice, encouragement and work with same-sex binational couples and LGBT and HIV-positive immigrants. We also thank former interns Tara Polansky, Fadi Hanna, and Aaron Morris for their contributions to drafts of this report. We give our deep thanks to Rachel B. Tiven, Victoria Neilson, Sarah Sohn, and Adam Pedersen-Doherty for their support in publishing this report.

Immigration Equality expresses deep appreciation to those who have made our work possible: the Arcus Foundation; the Evelyn and Walter Haas Jr., Fund; the Ford Foundation; the Open Society Institute; and the Paul Rapoport Foundation.

Human Rights Watch and Immigration Equality thank Congressman Jerrold Nadler and his staff, along with Senator Leahy and his staff, for their leadership in Congress struggling for justice for same-sex binational couples and LGBT immigrants and their families.

Human Rights Watch and Immigration Equality wish to acknowledge gratefully the work of the many organizations and individuals supporting the rights of binational same-sex couples. For their advice, insight and wisdom, we particularly thank: Anna Browne of Bay Area Immigrant Rights Coalition; Nancy Buermeyer, Cerissa Cafasso, and Mark Glaze of The Raben Group; Cathy Chang and the members of Las Buenas Amigas; Debanuj Dasgupta of the Queer Immigrant Rights Project; Marta Donayre and Leslie Bulbuk of Love Sees No Borders; Jennifer Hope of CUNY Law School; Mark Kightlinger; Martha McDevitt-Pugh of Love Exiles; Matthew McTighe of the Human Rights Campaign; Andrew Park; Roberta Sklar of the National Gay and Lesbian Task Force; and Paul Zakrzewski.. Human Rights Watch and Immigration Equality offer our gratitude and thanks to Steptoe and Johnson, LLC; William Isasi; and our colleagues in Brazil, Sonia Correa, Roger Raupp Rios, and Beto de Jesus for their research on global same-sex immigration rights. We thank Gary Gates for his thorough research into same-sex binational couples according to the 2000 U.S. Census. Human Rights Watch and Immigration Equality thank Chris Daley of the Transgender Law Center, Shannon Minter of the National Center for Lesbian Rights, and Cole Thaler of Lambda Legal Defense and Education Fund, for their guidance on transgender issues in immigration. We also thank Sebastian Cordoba, Machu Latorre and Tracey Luszcz for their visual expertise and support.

For their participation in a conference call during the developmental stages of this report, Human Rights Watch and Immigration Equality wish to thank: Dusty Aráujo, International Gay & Lesbian Human Rights Commission; Leslie Bulbuk, Love Sees No Borders; Jason Cianciotto, National Gay & Lesbian Task Force; Marta Donayre, Love Sees No Borders; Gary Gates, UCLA School of Law - The Williams Institute; Ariel Herrera, Amnesty International - Outfront; Steven Kang, Gay Asian Pacific Islander Men of New York; Davina Kotulsky, Marriage Equality U.S.A.; Martha McDevitt-Pugh, Love Exiles; and Matt McTighe, Human Rights Campaign.

Finally, we acknowledge the groundbreaking work of Lionel Cantu. Mr. Cantu's research on the impact of sexuality and migration within Mexican men-who-have-sex-with-men communities was highly influential in this report. We also thank Nancy Naples for her support and efforts to continue Lionel's work. Lionel Cantu died unexpectedly in Santa Cruz on May 26, 2002. We hope this report will help sustain his legacy and work.

This report is for the thousands of binational same-sex couples who struggle under the devastating burdens of U.S. immigration policy and non-recognition of their relationships for a simple wish: to be loving families with one another.

The first time that I dreamed, we were in flight. …
We came at once to a tall house, its door
Wide open, waiting for the long-lost heirs.
An elderly clerk sat on the bedroom stairs
Writing; but we had tiptoed past him when
He raised his head and stuttered: "Go away."
We wept and begged to stay;
He wiped his pince-nez, hesitated, then
Said no, he had no power to give us leave:
Our lives were not in order; we must leave.

W. H. Auden, "The Lesson"

I love my partner with every thing in me. … Thanks to the immigration laws they have taken my dreams and my heart and thrown them to the wind. I always thought when I found the love of my life, the only approval I would have ever cared about was of my mom and dad. Who would have thought that I needed the government to tell me that I can *only* fall in love here in the United States and even here I don't have a choice. The heart has no boundaries, it merely goes where it is loved.

E-mail from "Denise" (a clerk at Wal-Mart in Louisiana), forced to live on a different continent from her Dutch partner "Karla"

Table of Contents

Glossary

Immigration-Related Terms

Asylum: in the immigration context, safe haven provided to an individual who has a reasonable fear of persecution on account of race, religion, political opinion, national origin, or membership in a particular social group. An individual must ordinarily be present in the United States to apply for asylum there.

B-1 visa: a visitor's visa for business. These visas are available for up to six months for persons entering the United States to conduct business affairs such as: consulting with clients, meeting with business associates or attending professional, scientific or religious conventions. B-1 visitors are allowed to receive money for expenses in the U.S., but they cannot be paid a salary by an employer in this country.

B-2 visa: a visitor's visa for pleasure. These visas are available for a stay of up to six months for persons entering the United States for reasons of leisure or pleasure such as: tourism, amusement, visiting friends or relatives, rest, medical treatment, or activities of a social or service nature. The B-2 visa can also be used by a non-spousal partner (including a same-sex partner) of the holder of certain other visas to visit them in the United States.

Consular processing: the issuance of visas through foreign-based U.S. consulates.

Employment-based immigrant visa: a visa allowing indefinite or permanent stay in the United States based on employment. The Immigration and Nationality Act provides a yearly minimum of 140,000 employment-based immigrant visas divided into five preference categories. They may require a labor certification from the U.S. Department of Labor, and may require filing a petition with the Bureau of Citizenship and Immigration Services (previously INS).

Family-based visa: a visa allowing for the immigration of a foreigner to the United States based on relationship to a U.S. citizen or legal permanent resident.

F-1 visa: a visa available to full-time students who are admitted to an academic or language training program. Applicants must provide proof of the financial support needed for educational and living expenses, must retain a residence outside the U.S., and cannot work more than twenty hours a week at an on-campus job or spend more than one year of practical training after completion of courses. The U.S. government may issue additional employment authorization to students if severe unforeseen economic hardships arise after coming to the U.S.

Green card: a visa for permanent residence in the United States. This visa was once issued on green paper.

H-1B visa: a visa available to "specialty occupation workers," including fashion models or professionals who hold a license necessary to practice their profession in the U.S.

Hybrid visa: a non-immigrant visa with a path to permanent residency as part of its terms. Examples include the fiancé(e) or K visa.

Immigrant: an individual who enters the United States with authorization from the government to remain on a permanent basis.

Immigrant intent: the motivation of a person who is present in the United States on a temporary basis, but intends to remain beyond the legally authorized validity of the visa.

Immigrant visa: authorization from the United States government to remain in the U.S. on an indefinite or permanent basis.

Immigration and Nationality Act (INA): also known as the McCarran-Walter Act, the 1952 INA collected and codified many existing provisions and organized the structure of immigration law. Before the INA, a variety of statutes governed immigration but were not organized in one location. Amended many times over the years, the Act remains the basic body of immigration law. It established family reunification as a central goal of U.S. immigration policy.

J-visa: a visa available to trainees, students, professors, research scholars, non-academic specialists, foreign physicians, au pairs, and summer students in travel/work programs. Some visa recipients must return to the country of their last residence for two years after their visa expires before obtaining any subsequent visas.

K-1 visa: a visa available to the fiancé(e) of a United States citizen. K-visa holders must marry within ninety days after admission to the United States. K-2 visas are available to K-1 visa holders' minor children.

K-3 visa: a visa available to persons who have a valid marriage to a U.S. citizen and who have filed for, but not yet received, permanent residence in the United States.

Naturalization: the process by which U.S. citizenship is conferred on a foreign citizen or national after he or she fulfills the requirements established in the Immigration and Nationality Act (INA). Requirements for administrative naturalization include showing:

- a period of continuous residence and physical presence in the United States;
- an ability to read, write, and speak English;
- a knowledge and understanding of U.S. history and government;
- good moral character;
- attachment to the principles of the U.S. Constitution;
- favorable disposition toward the United States.

Non-immigrant: a person who is authorized to remain in the United States on a temporary basis only.

Non-immigrant visa: permission by the government to remain in the United States for a termed or temporary period.

Removal proceedings: process by which the government formally ends a person's access to the United States. Part of the process includes returning an individual to his or her native country.

Undocumented immigrant: a person who is present in the United States without proper authorization.

Other Terms

Biological sex: the biological classification of bodies as male or female, based on factors including external sex organs, internal sexual and reproductive organs, hormones, and chromosomes.

Bisexual: a person who is attracted to both sexes.

Gay: a synonym for homosexual. Sometimes used to describe only males who are attracted primarily to other males.

Gender: the social and cultural codes used to distinguish between what a society considers "masculine" or "feminine" conduct.

Gender divergent: a term used to refer to a person who does not conform either to expectations for their assigned sex or to the binary nature of male and female gender assignments.

Gender expression: the external characteristics and behaviors which societies define as "masculine" or "feminine"—including such attributes as dress, appearance, mannerisms, speech patterns, and social behavior and interactions.

Gender identity: a person's internal, deeply felt sense of being male or female, or something other than or in between male and female.

Heterosexual: a person attracted primarily to people of the opposite sex.

HIV: human immunodeficiency virus, the virus which causes Acquired Immune Deficiency Syndrome (AIDS).

HIV-positive: a term used for a person who has tested positive for antibodies to the HIV virus, indicating exposure to the virus.

Homosexual: a person attracted primarily to people of the same sex.

Lesbian: a female attracted primarily to other females.

LGBT: lesbian, gay, bisexual or transgender; an inclusive term for groups and identities sometimes also associated together as "sexual minorities."

Queer: often used as a slur in English to refer to lesbian, gay, bisexual, and transgender persons, the term "queer" has been reclaimed by many people in the U.S. and other countries as an expression of pride in one's sexual orientation and gender identity.

Same-sex: term often used to describe the relationships of lesbian, gay, bisexual and sometimes transgender people.

Serostatus: a positive or negative reaction to a test on one's blood serum for signs of disease or of antibodies to disease—often used to describe whether one has tested positive for antibodies to HIV.

Sexual orientation: the way in which a person's sexual and emotional desires are directed. The term categorizes according to the sex of the object of desire—that is, it describes whether a person is attracted primarily toward people of the same or opposite sex or to both.

Transgender: one whose inner gender identity or outward gender expression differs from the physical characteristics of their body at birth. Female-to-male (FTM) transgender people were born with female bodies but have a predominantly male gender identity; male-to-female (MTF) transgender people were born with male bodies but have a predominantly female gender identity.

Transsexual: one who has undergone surgery and hormone therapies (processes sometimes called "sex reassignment surgery") to make his/her physical sex correspond more closely to his/her internal gender identity.

I. Belonging

Summary

Who belongs?

The United States is peopled by the displaced and exiled, and divided by belonging. Who is inside and who outside; whom the government recognizes and whom it rejects, have been basic questions through its history. The ramifications reach into the realms of intimacy. When two people fall in love and plan to live the rest of their lives together, they may depend on the state to acknowledge and safeguard their union: never more so than if they have different nationalities. United States policy is to help foreign spouses and fiancé(e)s immigrate and live with their U.S. partners. But not if that partner is of the same sex.

Binational same-sex partnerships are lesbian and gay couples where one partner is a U.S. citizen or permanent resident, the other a foreign national.[1] In 2000, the U.S. Census, investigating household makeup, estimated 35,820 such couples lived together in the United States. This represented some 6% of all lesbian or gay couples counted in the country. These couples dwell in every state, make their way at every income level, represent a mosaic of American diversity. The foreign-national partners come from almost every nation in the world.

Their relationships have no recognition in federal law, and no rights.

These figures only suggest the issue's scope. They do not count couples who hide the fact that they are partners, lest the one applying to stay face homophobia in the immigration or asylum process. They do not count couples who avoid the census, because the foreign partner lives here illegally to maintain the relationship, or fears being forced to do so after a visa expires. They do not count couples who do not share a home—or who live in different countries because U.S. immigration law, and marriage policy, will not permit them to share their lives together within its borders. They do not count couples where the U.S. partner has chosen exile, so that they can lead common

[1] The term "lesbian and gay" is frequently used in this report to refer to people whose identities--or behaviors and desires--could be variously described as lesbian, gay, bisexual, or transgender. This term is used to minimize reducing people's identities to an alphabetical acronym, "LGBT", and is used for simplicity and convenience. Its use should not imply that the couples whose stories are told here do not include bisexual or transgender people.

lives in another, friendlier country than this one. (At least nineteen countries have acknowledged lesbian and gay relationships in immigration law and policy, while the U.S. still refuses. See Appendix B for more information.)

Undoubtedly the more than 70,000 members of such families whom the last census counted are only a part, perhaps a very small one, of the whole.

This report documents the crippling barriers such families face in pursuing a goal enshrined in America's founding document—happiness. Those barriers center around a simple fact. With only rare exceptions, a heterosexual couple where one partner is foreign, one a U.S. citizen, can claim the right to enter the U.S. with a few strokes of a pen.[2] They need not even marry: they need only show to a U.S. consulate abroad that they *intend* to do so and have met at least once before in their lives. (Waivers of the latter rule are possible.)

In practice, U.S. immigration is filled with obstacles for many who seek to enter. Any binational family may encounter injustices and bureaucratic barriers on the road to reunification. A flawed and irrational system demands overhaul. But a lesbian or gay couple cannot even claim basic rights. Their relationship—even if they have lived together for decades, even if their commitment is incontrovertible and public, even if they have married or formalized their partnership in a place where that is possible—is irrelevant for purposes of entering the United States. Instead, they face a long limbo of legal indifference, harassment, and fear. Couples told us stories of abuse by immigration officials, and even deportation. They described the devastating impact not only on their partnerships but on their careers, homes, children, livelihoods, and lives.

An American man, faced with the expiration of his Venezuelan partner's tourist visa, wrote us:

> I am very proud to be an AMERICAN. … We are trying to find other options to allow Jorge to stay in the country—we do not know what options we have but with our faith in God—we believe we will find the answers. I respect the laws of the United States and will continue to do so if Jorge's visa expires. …. We have no intention to break up or separate—this is not an option—it has never been an option for the

---

[2] Most exceptions involve cases where U.S. law applies special rules to nationals of a particular country. For the consequences of one such instance, see "Families Torn Apart: The High Cost of U.S. and Cuban Travel Restrictions," A Human Rights Watch Report, October 2005, vol.17, no. 5 (B).

> heterosexual couples Jorge dreams about being an American citizen, celebrating the incredible freedom afforded to Americans, and to once again be proud of a country he strongly believes in.[3]

Some couples find such stubborn confidence impossible. A woman in Iowa, living with her partner from New Zealand, wrote that immigration laws:

> do not allow my partner to live a free life, she is in constant fear of being deported and removed from this country and her family. We live a struggle every day as there is only one income. Together we are raising a twelve-year old son. Nadia, my partner, is my son's mother also, and losing her would destroy that little boy's life, she is just as much a part of him as I am. She keeps this family together and whole. I am also a veteran of the United States Navy and have done my time and service to my country. It breaks my heart that for all I've done with this country it will not see the person I love who has strength to hold me up when life is bad—she cannot remain even after the commitment we have put into each other and our son's life. I cannot imagine life without her. How could anyone live without their heart.[4]

Many couples are separated, many families broken up. A woman in North Carolina described how her Hungarian partner and the children they were raising together were forced to leave the country.

> Even though the children went to school here and grew up here and this is Home! It's just not right. No family should be forced to be apart no matter what the sex is. It's all for love. No one should determine how to live your life like this, no one. This is how immigration laws have affected us. We are separated, and without each other… We just want to be together, that's all. No harm in that.[5]

Over and over couples spoke of the contradiction between what they thought were American values and the reality they know. Liz, divided from her Jamaican partner

---

[3] E-mail to Immigration Equality from Shaine (last name withheld at his request), November 6, 2003.

[4] E-mail to Immigration Equality from Cara and Nadia (names changed at their request), September 13, 2003.

[5] E-mail to Immigration Equality from Sandra (last name withheld at her request), October 29, 2005.

Carly, said, "I have a right to pursue happiness and Carly makes me happy. We don't hurt anyone. … That's all."[6]

Many U.S. citizens go into exile to preserve their families and stay with their life partners. One man, living an ocean away from his Portuguese partner, said:

> The U.S. government does not want to acknowledge that homosexuals are entitled to be happy, just as any human beings… Now that I have finally found my soul mate, the U.S. government wants to tell me that I do not have the right to be with him. If immigration laws don't change in the near future, I will be leaving the United States, even if that means being unemployed and living in misery. At least I'll be with the one I love.[7]

A U.S. woman who has moved to Denmark to be with her partner of almost twenty years told us, "It was a lot of letting go. I had to give up my career; I had to give up my country. But I gained a lot too. I gained the recognition of our union here. I would never go back on a decision that allowed us to have and to raise our two wonderful kids."[8]

Family reunification is an express and central goal of U.S. immigration policy, and has been for more than fifty years. Immigration law puts priority on allowing citizens and permanent residents to sponsor their spouses and relatives for entry into the U.S.[9] A commission appointed by Congress to study immigration policies in 1981 concluded:

> Reunification of families serves the national interest not only through the humaneness of the policy itself, but also through the promotion of the public order and well-being of the nation. Psychologically and

---

[6] Human Rights Watch interview with Liz and Carly (names changed at their request), New York, February 10, 2005.

[7] E-mail to Immigration Equality from Rafael (last name withheld at his request), undated, 2003.

[8] Human Rights Watch/Immigration Equality telephone interview with Gitte and Kelly Bossi-Andresen, December 20, 2005.

[9] "Immediate relatives" of U.S. citizens are exempt from quotas and generally processed quickly through the immigration system; these include spouses and minor children of U.S. citizens, and parents of U.S. citizens who are over twenty-one. There are also "family preference" immigration categories. These include adult children and siblings of U.S. citizens, and spouses, minor children, and adult unmarried children of lawful permanent residents. In these cases there are severe backlogs, and waiting lines of years.

socially, the reunion of family members … promotes the health and welfare of the United States.[10]

But, lesbian and gay people's families do not count. Their partners are excluded from the definition of "spouse."

Such couples are trapped between two ferocious panics sweeping the U.S. One is over equality in civil marriage. Amid rancorous debate about whether to recognize lesbian and gay people's partnerships at any level, some distort the demand for simple fairness into a claim for "special rights," and portray the principle of non-discrimination as a bid for privilege. Some opponents of "gay marriage" openly define lesbian, gay, bisexual, and transgender people themselves as second-class citizens. One makes clear that homosexuals are not only unequal but "unqualified" to participate in society's basic benefits:

> Homosexual marriage will devalue your marriage. A license to marry is a legal document by which government will treat same-sex marriage as if it were equal to the real thing. A license speaks for the government and will tell society that government says the marriages are equal. Any time a lesser thing is made equal to a greater, the greater is devalued. … Granting a marriage license to homosexuals because they engage in sex is as illogical as granting a medical license to a barber because he wears a white coat or a law license to a salesman because he carries a briefcase. Real doctors, lawyers, and the public would suffer as a result of licensing the unqualified and granting them rights, benefits, and responsibilities.[11]

The fear of what one writer called "ceremonialization of anal sodomy"[12] led in 1996 to the so-called Defense of Marriage Act. Limited local recognition of same-sex partnerships already had no effect on immigration policy, which is a federal concern.

---

[10] See U.S. Select Committee on Immigration and Refugee Policy, "U.S. Immigration Policy and the National Interest" (1981), p. 112, quoted in Chris Duenas, "Coming to America: The Immigration Obstacle Facing Binational Same-Sex Couples," *Southern California Law Review*, vol. 73 (2000), pp. 811–841. See also Linda Kelly, "Preserving the Fundamental Right to Family Unity: Championing Notions of Social Contract and Community Ties in the Battle of Plenary Power Versus Aliens' Rights," *Villanova Law Review,* vol. 41 (1996), pp. 725, 729.

[11] Jan LaRue, "Talking Points: Why Homosexual 'Marriage' is Wrong," Concerned Women for America, September 16, 2003, at http://www.cwfa.org/articledisplay.asp?id=4589&department=LEGAL&categoryid=family (retrieved January 10, 2005).

[12] John Haskins, "'Conservative' Romney buckles and blunders," World Net Daily, December 24, 2005, at http://www.worldnetdaily.com/news/article.asp?ARTICLE_ID=48056 (retrieved January 4, 2006).

The Defense of Marriage Act, however, declared that for all purposes of the federal government, marriage would mean "only a legal union between one man and one woman as husband and wife." The exclusion of lesbian and gay couples from U.S. family-reunification policy was written unequivocally into law.

Binational couples, along with tens of thousands of other non-citizens, also face the rising panic over immigration in the U.S. That exclusionary impulse is nothing new. A conservative who calls immigration "the most immediate and most serious challenge to America's traditional identity"[13] echoes, perhaps unwittingly, nativist rhetoric more than a century and a half old. After the September 11, 2001 attacks, cultural difference was increasingly seen as criminal threat. Foreign visitors and immigrants became "the single greatest threat to the lives of America's 280 million people."[14] Polemicists dubbed the Mexican border "Terrorist Alley." Politicians complained that taxpayers had to pay to bury undocumented immigrants who expired trekking across the desert (saying immigration "imposes incredible financial strains—sometimes in the least likely ways")[15] yet also objected to systems allowing those aliens to signal for help before dying of thirst ("Could there be a more blatant slap in the face of American taxpayers than to have them fund such disgraceful boondoggles?")[16]

Lesbian, gay, bisexual, and transgender foreigners share the spreading stigma and, like other non-nationals, encounter locked doors—and cells. In December 2005, the House of Representatives passed the "Border Protection, Antiterrorism & Illegal Immigration Control Act." The bill, and similar proposals, would criminalize undocumented immigrants and those who help them. "Unlawful presence," now a civil immigration violation, would become a crime subject to state and local police pursuit. An undocumented immigrant would be barred from seeking asylum, and their detention would be mandatory. [17]

An immigrant could fall victim to this provision one day after a visa expires. Student visa holders would be at risk if they dropped below required course loads. And anyone who

---

[13] Samuel P. Huntington,"The Hispanic Challenge," *Foreign Policy*, No. 142 (March/April 2004), pp. 30-45.

[14] John Perazzo, "Illegal Immigration and Terrorism," *Front Page Magazine,* December 18, 2002, at http://www.frontpagemag.com/Articles/ReadArticle.asp?ID=5147 (retrieved January 5, 2005).

[15] Webpage of the House Immigration Reform Caucus, at www.house.gov/tancredo/Immigration/WYB.2004.09.29.html (retrieved December 15, 2005).

[16] John Perazzo, "Illegal Immigration and Terrorism," Front Page Magazine, December 18, 2002, at http://www.frontpagemag.com/Articles/ReadArticle.asp?ID=5147, (retrieved January 5, 2005).

[17] See "Oppose the Border Protection, Antiterrorism, and Illegal Immigration Control Act: Letter to House Judiciary Committee Members opposing HR 4437," Human Rights Watch, December 7, 2005, at http://hrw.org/english/docs/2005/12/09/usdom12188.htm.

knowingly tries to help a foreigner in this predicament could become a criminal. Many binational lesbian and gay couples could be injured. A U.S. citizen whose same-sex partner became undocumented could be convicted of "smuggling" them—and imprisoned, and stripped of home and property.

Recommendations

Freedom from discrimination is a human right. The hardship, harassment, and pain that same-sex binational couples endure in confronting and trying to conform to U.S. law show the discriminatory consequences of denying a class of people the recognition their relationships need and deserve.

Equally important, the losses and separations also reflect a broken immigration system: inconsistent standards, processes ridden with arbitrariness and delay, a ramshackle set of often conflicting rules which encourage discrimination and abuse. Innumerable families negotiating the U.S.'s reunification system find enormous impediments to living together in this country. The problems of lesbian and gay couples are only one aspect of the system's failures. As one gay Argentinean and his American partner told us, ruefully: "Bureaucracy doesn't move at the pace of people's lives."[18]

Once again, though, while heterosexual families can elicit a measure of public and political sympathy, the animus against lesbian and gay families is embodied in law. Even their claim to family status is foreclosed from the start. The United States urgently needs to enact comprehensive immigration reform—ensuring adequate and fair avenues for immigrants to enter the United States both temporarily and permanently and offering reasonable roads to legal status for undocumented immigrants already living and working in the country. Ending the egregious discrimination that excludes lesbian and gay families from reunification policies must be part of that.

Traditionally, the Supreme Court has accorded Congress wide scope to regulate entry to the U.S., holding it is part of the "plenary powers" given the legislature by the U.S. Constitution. This power is not absolute, though, or completely immune from scrutiny for discrimination and injustice. The Court has acknowledged cases "in which the alleged basis of discrimination is so outrageous" that denial of entry may be challenged—including denying people entry solely because of their race or religion.[19]

---

[18] Human Rights Watch/Immigration Equality telephone interview with Fabian and Robert (last names withheld at their request), October 6, 2005.

[19] *Reno v American-Arab Anti-Discrimination Committee,* Supreme Court of the United States, 5525 U.S. 471 (1999) at 491.

Moreover, it is important to stress that all immigrants on U.S. soil—including those here illegally—are guaranteed the same rights as citizens, with only a few exceptions, such as the right to vote. The U.S. Constitution grants to "the people" or "persons"—not just to citizens—the rights to due process and equal protection of the law, to be free from arbitrary detention or cruel and unusual punishment.

Yet U.S. citizens (and permanent residents) are equally victims along with their foreign-national partners. Solely because of their sexual orientation or gender identity, they find their relationships unrecognized, their families endangered, their lives shadowed by separation and dislocation. Often, their relationships are wrecked, or driven underground.

The philosopher Tzvetan Todorov (writing in an altogether different context) has tried to define "dignity," vital among the panoply of values that make up human rights. He finds it connected to the human ability to make meaningful decisions about one's own life and to make these decisions known. "The important thing is to act out the strength of one's own will, to exert through one's initiative some influence, however minimal, on one's surroundings. ... It is not enough simply *to decide* to acquire dignity: that decision must give rise to an act that is visible to others (even if they are not actually there to see it). This can be one definition of dignity."[20] Denying recognition to one of the most important choices a human being can make, forcing the relationship consequent on that decision into terrified invisibility—these assault human dignity in an essential way.

Human Rights Watch and Immigration Equality both strongly support full equality in civil marriage, allowing same-sex couples the same recognition under law that heterosexual couples enjoy. Together we regard discrimination in the legal recognition of relationships as a gross violation of human rights.[21]

However, repairing the inequity in the immigration system that tears same-sex binational families apart is an issue distinct from the debate over same-sex marriage. Many other countries which have accorded immigration rights to such couples have done so separately from enacting civil partnerships or opening marriage status.

---

[20] Tzvetan Todorov, *Facing the Extreme* (New York: Henry Holt, 1996), p. 61.

[21] See "Non-Discrimination in Civil Marriage: Perspectives from International Human Rights Law and Practice," a Human Rights Watch briefing paper, September 3, 2003, at http://hrw.org/backgrounder/lgbt/civil-marriage.htm.

Acknowledging this discrimination as a remediable failure of the immigration system is the aim of a bill now before Congress. The Uniting American Families Act (UAFA) would add the category "permanent partner" to the classes of family members entitled to sponsor a foreign national for U.S. immigration.

The UAFA would not grant couples recognition or rights for any purposes other than immigration. Nor is it likely to open the gates to waves of newcomers. The figure of almost 40,000 binational lesbian and gay couples whom the census discovered represents a significant population suffering serious harm—but it hardly suggests that legal recognition would add more than minimally to the number of immigrants (between 700,000 and one million) whom the U.S. already admits yearly.[22] People claiming permanent partnership would have to prove the fact, and undergo the same rigorous investigations that authorities already impose on binational married couples—meaning the bill would not open new possibilities for "marriage fraud."

Rather, the bill would address an egregious inequality. It would protect dedicated families and their children. It would prevent the drain of talented people to other countries. Its passage is urgent. (A full description of the UAFA is found in Appendix A.)

Human Rights Watch and Immigration Equality call on the United States Congress to:

- Enact the Uniting American Families Act so that binational same-sex couples' relationships receive the same recognition and treatment currently enjoyed by binational married couples within the current U.S. immigration policy providing for family unification.

- Repeal the Federal Defense of Marriage Act (DOMA) which mandates discriminatory treatment of lesbian and gay relationships by the U.S. federal government. Until the DOMA is repealed, eliminate discrimination against lesbian and gay couples by prohibiting DOMA application in the context of U.S. immigration law and administrative regulations.

---

[22] Recent annual figures number 849,807 for 2000; 1,064,318 for 2001; 1,063,732 for 2002; and 705,827 for 2003. See the *Fiscal Year 2003 Yearbook of Immigration Statistics,* online at http://uscis.gov/graphics/shared/aboutus/statistics/IMM03yrbk/IMMExcel/Table01.xls (retrieved December 15, 2005).

- Fashion any reforms to U.S. immigration law to guarantee respect for all human and labor rights of non-citizens. Ensure that any immigration reforms do not have the effect of discriminating against persons on the basis of race, color, descent, religion, gender, health status, sexual orientation, gender identity, or national or ethnic origin.[23]

- In accordance with International Guidelines on HIV/AIDS and Human Rights (UNHCHR/UNAIDS, 1998; para.105), stating that "there is no public health rationale for restricting liberty of movement or choice of residence on the grounds of HIV status," amend the Immigration and Nationality Act Section 212(a)(1)(i) to declassify HIV as a "communicable disease of public health significance," which renders HIV-positive citizens non-admissible without seeking a discretionary waiver. (See chapters II and VI for detailed information.)

Human Rights Watch and Immigration Equality call on the United States Department of Homeland Security, the Attorney General of the United States, and the U.S. Department of State to:

- End discrimination against same-sex couples throughout the immigration process, ensuring that the burden of proof in determining the validity of same-sex partnerships is comparable to that of heterosexual partnerships.

- As an overarching matter of priority, ensure that wherever family ties would be taken into consideration in the U.S. immigration process, relationships between same-sex partners count on an equal basis with heterosexual relationships. This non-discrimination standard should be applied *inter alia* whenever the Department of Homeland Security, the Attorney General of the United States, or the U.S. Department of State:
    - determines eligibility for bond on post-order custody reviews;
    - considers cancellation of removal applications, extreme hardship waivers, and similar applications and decisions;
    - recognizes the status of a couple entering the United States on the I-94 customs declaration;
    - makes consular decisions on visa eligibility based on family relationships.

---

[23] For the national origin aspect of this recommendation, see U.N. Committee on the Elimination of Racial Discrimination, General Recommendation 30, CERD/C/64/Misc.11/rev.3, March 2004.

Human Rights Watch and Immigration Equality call on the United States Department of Homeland Security to:

- Ensure that the burden of proof in determining the validity of same-sex partnerships is comparable to that of heterosexual partnerships.
- Allow non-immigrant visa holders to bring same-sex partners as dependents of the primary visa holder during the duration of the primary visa holder's stay.
- Allow same-sex partnerships legally recognized in foreign or domestic jurisdictions to be legally valid for U.S. immigration purposes.
- Ensure that same-sex couples are able to enter the U.S. as couples on the I-94 customs declaration, rather than as single entrants.
- Implement training to counter discrimination based on sexual orientation or gender identity or expression in all areas of the immigration system. This should be provided to employees of all ranks and be given at regular intervals, not merely at the start of employment. External instructors and community organizations should be engaged for training.
- Ensure that all non-citizens facing removal from the United States have access to judicial review and appeal to a higher authority, as required by international human rights law. In addition, ensure that detained individuals, including those detained pending deportation, have access to judicial review of the decision to detain.
- Amend the Detention Operations Manual—including the Disciplinary Procedures, Section IIIA(5)(b) and Detainee Classification System, Section IIID—to prohibit any discrimination against protections for the health and safety of vulnerable groups, including lesbian, gay, bisexual, and transgender people, and people living with HIV/AIDS.
- Ensure that the Detainee Grievance Procedures of the Detention Operations Manual are implemented in a manner that prohibits and prevents discrimination against vulnerable groups, including lesbian, gay, bisexual, and transgender people, and people living with HIV/AIDS.

- Implement a central, accessible, and up-to-date system of complaint for incidents of harassment and discrimination by immigration officials. Complaint mechanisms must be multilingual. Complaints should be promptly and impartially investigated. Individuals who bring complaints must be protected from intimidation and repercussions. Individuals who have brought claims of abuse should have the option of appealing their case.

II. Sex and Security: A Short History of Exclusions

Richard Adams, a United States citizen, was in love with Anthony Sullivan, an Australian national. They lived together in Colorado in 1975. With Anthony's visa about to expire, Adams tried to sponsor him for permanent residency in the U.S. The written answer of the Immigration and Naturalization Service made its position clear:

> Your visa petition…for classification of Anthony Corbett Sullivan as the spouse of a United States citizen [is] denied for the following reasons: *You have failed to establish that a bona fide marital relationship can exist between two faggots.* [24]

Three decades later, what has changed? "Faggot" relationships remain fake within the system. And even the word resurfaces. One man wrote us:

> While traveling abroad I met the person I would spend the rest of my life with, and eventually start a family with. Bogdan is a citizen of … the former Yugoslavia. Because of both of our countries' treatment [of] its own gay citizens, it's been impossible to be together at some points. Most of the time I've had to go to Serbia, because after Bogdan tried obtaining a visa at the American Embassy in Belgrade, he was denied, because "they don't give visas to fag couples," as we were told by the visa officer. … I, being an American, had the preconception that my country was the true land of the free. I guess I was wrong.[25]

Immigration, Gender, and Sexuality in U.S. History

Lesbian or gay non-citizens trying to join their U.S. partners, and transgender people trying to see their relationships acknowledged, are caught between two forces: escalating panic about "porous" borders, and intensifying battles over the legal status of partnerships between people of the same sex.

---

[24] Letter from Immigration and Naturalization Service to Richard Adams (Nov. 24, 1975) (in Stephen H. Legomsky, *Immigration and Refugee Law and Policy* 139, 2nd ed. 1997).

[25] E-mail to Immigration Equality (names withheld or changed at the author's request), May 29, 2005.

These pincers convey an unmistakable message: *You do not belong.* Yet neither ferocious anti-immigrant feeling, nor fear of sexuality and sexual "deviance," is new in U.S. politics or society. Nor is it novel for them to meet.

The United States has long been schizophrenic about its own immigrant identity. In the nineteenth century, the U.S. had land, and needed labor. Early immigrants such as the Irish might face invective and violence, but rarely had to hurdle major legal barriers at the ports where they disembarked.[26] The numbers rose; their sources shifted, from northern to southern and eastern Europe.[27] From 1860 to 1920, almost thirty million immigrants entered the country, invigorating every part of the nation's life from literature to cuisine, infusing its culture with their cultures, increasing its population, wealth, and power.[28] Yet, hostility reared to meet them. In the 1880s, as Emma Lazarus famously imagined the Statue of Liberty offering luminous asylum to tired and poor beside the "Golden Door," that anger showed ominous strength.

The rage involved fears about reproduction: that newcomers—whom one politician called "the ignorant, lawless, idle and dangerous overflow of all other countries"[29]—would outbreed Anglo-Saxons. It involved fears about gender: that promiscuous immigrant cultures would erode masculinity and femininity in the middle-class U.S.

Fantasies about immigrants' sexualities figured heavily in anti-immigrant prejudice—from pornographic imprecations against Irish convents as scenes for orgies[30] to a lurid literature on "white slavery."[31] At the end of the nineteenth century, these bogeymen

---

[26] See John Higham's magisterial *Strangers in the Land: Patterns of American Nativism, 1860-1925* (New York: Atheneum, 1973). That said, the very first immigration law passed by the U.S. Congress in 1790 had limited entry to "free white" persons. Nor should the power of prejudice and violence against immigrants in the first half of the century be underestimated.

[27] Immigration from Asia also increased, and encountered particularly savage racism.

[28] Table, "Immigration to the United States: Fiscal Years 1820-2004," in *Yearbook of Immigration Statistics: 2004,* at http://uscis.gov/graphics/shared/statistics/yearbook/2004/table1.xls (retrieved February 9, 2006).

[29] Tammany politician George W. Curtis, quoted in Higham, p. 41.

[30] Martha Butt Sherwood's *The Nun,* published in the U.S. in 1834, was an early tract claiming that convents were virtual brothels; it helped incite an enraged nativist mob to burn an Ursuline convent in Charlestown, Massachusetts the same year. Other scandalous volumes, such as *The Awful Disclosures of Maria Monk, as Exhibited in a Narrative of Her Sufferings During a Residence of Five Years as a Novice and Two Years as a Black Nun, in the Hotel Dieu Nunnery in Montreal* (published in 1836) fed anti-Irish and anti-Catholic sentiment throughout the century. See Marie Anne Pagliarini, "The Pure American Woman and the Wicked Catholic Priest: An Analysis of Anti-Catholic Literature in Antebellum America," *Religion and American Culture*, vol. 9, no. 1 (Winter, 1999), pp. 97-128.

[31] An inflammatory and extensive campaign excited racist fears by charging immigrants with smuggling European women into the United States, or American women abroad, and forcing them into sex work—so-called "white slavery."

took on both legal and scientific garb. The 1875 Page Act was the first major federal measure restricting entry; prostitutes were a key category of "undesirables" it excluded, and sensational stories about sex workers from China led to further bans on Chinese immigration.[32] Meanwhile, Francis Walker, an influential statistician and superintendent of two successive U.S. censuses, warned of "immigrants from southern Italy, Hungary, Austria, and Russia" who "are beaten men from beaten races; representing the worst failures in the struggle for existence."[33] Yet he saw weaklings paradoxically weakening their betters. If the "older stock" of Americans lost ground to the invaders, it was because the latecomers actually *caused a declining birthrate* among the "native-born":

> The appearance of vast numbers of men … with habits repellent to our native people, of an industrial grade suited only to the lowest kind of manual labor, was exactly such a cause as by any student of population would be expected to affect profoundly the growth of the native population. Americans … became increasingly unwilling to bring forth sons and daughters who should be obliged to compete in the market for labor and in the walks of life with those whom they did not recognize as of their own grade and condition.[34]

The eminent sociologist Edward A. Ross, in 1901, called it "race suicide":

> There is no bloodshed, no violence, no assault of the race that waxes upon the race that wanes. The higher race quietly and unmurmuringly eliminates itself rather than endure individually the bitter competition it has failed to ward off from itself by collective action.[35]

President Theodore Roosevelt popularized these ideas and prophesied America's eclipse through "the elimination instead of the survival of the fittest."[36]

---

[32] Eithne Luibheid, *Entry Denied: Controlling Sexuality at the Border* (Minneapolis: University of Minnesota, 2002), pp. 31-51. The Chinese Exclusion Act of 1882 imposed overtly racist restrictions on Asian immigration which were progressively tightened in succeeding revisions; it barred all Chinese immigrants from naturalization.

[33] Francis A. Walker, "Restriction of Immigration," *The Atlantic Monthly,* vol. 77, no. 464 (June 1896), pp. 822-829.

[34] Ibid.

[35] Edward A. Ross, "The Causes of Race Superiority," *Annals of the American Academy of Political and Social Science,* vol. 18 (1901), pp. 67-89.

[36] Theodore Roosevelt, "A Letter from President Roosevelt on Race Suicide," *American Monthly Review of Reviews*, vol. 35 (1907), p. 550.

Such racist notions played on a distorted Darwinism. Immigrants became a biological threat, defined by their prolific sexuality and perverse vigor. The emerging pseudo-science of eugenics—the belief that societies should keep the "unfit" from breeding—bolstered anti-immigrant sentiment.[37] Not only the crude rural racists of the Ku Klux Klan, but urban intellectuals and self-styled progressives argued that immigration and immigrants' reproduction had to stop.[38] Yet underlying all these fears was a deep cultural pessimism, a foreshadowing of doom—ill-at-ease with traditional American optimism, but shared by powerful politicians such as Henry Cabot Lodge as well as writers like Henry and Brooks Adams. One distinguished historian describes how the latter

> used to greet each day by singing a song of his own invention, which consisted entirely of three repeated words: "God damn it! God damn it! God damn it!" For these gentlemen, history was indeed one goddamned thing after another—a steady spiral running downward toward the left, and culminating in some dark catastrophe—lava flowing through the streets of Quincy, or a tidal wave crashing upon Nahant, or a wild-eyed mob of Jews and Irishmen smashing in the doors of the Boston Athenaeum and scribbling madly in the margins of books.[39]

Groups opposing immigration spread and spawned: a "Race Betterment Foundation," the "Committee on Selective Immigration," a "National Committee for Mental Hygiene."[40] The word "hygiene" is suggestive. Immigrants were a racial peril, but also a menace to healthy masculinity, enervating men of the "native stock." As one congressman said in 1896, immigration restriction was needed "to preserve the human blood *and manhood* of the American character by the exclusion of depraved human beings."[41] The proximity of immigrants, with their exuberant, excessive sexuality, jumbled gender relations—producing an "impotent, decadent manhood."[42]

---

[37] See Wendy Kline, *Building a Better Race: Gender, Sexuality, and Eugenics from the Turn of the Century to the Baby Boom* (Berkeley: University of California, 2001), which also traces ancestral connections between early "scientific racism" and contemporary movements to "defend the family."

[38] See Donald K. Pickens, *Eugenics and the Progressives* (Nashville: Vanderbilt University Press), 1968.

[39] David Hackett Fischer, *Historians' Fallacies: Toward a Logic of Historical Thought* (New York: Harper, 1970), p. 139.

[40] Annie L. Cot, "'Breed Out the Unfit and Breed In the Fit': Irving Fisher, Economics, and the Science of Heredity," *American Journal of Economics and Sociology*, vol. 64, no. 3 (July 2005).

[41] Congressman John Corliss, quoted in Jeanne Petit, "Breeders, Workers, and Mothers: Gender and the Congressional Literacy Test Debate, 1896-1897," *Journal of the Gilded Age and Progressive Era*, vol. 3, no. 1 (2004), emphasis added.

[42] Gail Bederman, *Manliness and Civilization: A Cultural History of Gender and Race in the United States, 1866-1917* (Chicago: University of Chicago Press, 1996), p. 200.

One historian suggests that "Working-class and immigrant men, as well as middle-class women, were challenging white middle-class men's beliefs that they were the ones who should control the nation's destiny":

> [P]olitics had been viewed as part of the male sphere, as an exclusively male bailiwick... As immigrants wrested political control from middle-class men in one city after another, a very real basis of urban middle-class men's manhood received both symbolic and material blows. Immigrant men's efforts to control urban politics were, in a very real sense, contests of manhood—contests which the immigrants frequently won.[43]

Madison Grant's dire and popular 1916 book *The Passing of the Great Race*, a kind of Brahmin *Mein Kampf,* mixed many of these themes, fulminating:

> We Americans must realize that the altruistic ideals which have controlled our social development during the past century, and the maudlin sentimentalism that has made America "an asylum for the oppressed," are sweeping the nation toward a racial abyss. If the Melting Pot is allowed to boil without control ...the type of native American of Colonial descent will become as extinct as the Athenian of the age of Pericles.[44]

And sexual "deviance" came from without. In 1907, a doctor wrote, "It scarcely needs to be mentioned that Americans frequently blame one or the other [immigrant] group for homosexuality."[45]

A sweeping "red scare" took place in 1919-1920, when a federal attorney general and an ambitious aide named J. Edgar Hoover warned that anarchist immigrants intended revolution—and deported hundreds. Existing fears thus drew new power from the specter of terrorism. From 1917, a new wave of laws restricted immigrant intake. They culminated in the Immigration Act of 1924. It clamped an overall numerical cap on immigration; national quotas within that figure were fixed according to percentages of national origin in the U.S. population. The framers particularly meant to choke the flow

---

[43] Ibid., pp.13-15.

[44] Madison Grant, *The Passing of the Great Race: Or the Racial Basis of Human History* (New York: Scribner's, 1916), p. 228.

[45] Dr. Charles H. Hughes, quoted in Luibheid, p. 14.

from southern and Eastern Europe; immigration from Italy, for instance, plummeted more than twentyfold, from over 200,000 in 1921 to just over 8,000 in 1926.[46] The act also effectively ended legal immigration from Asia. One triumphant nativist exulted at the time that it "marks the close of an epoch in the history of the United States."[47]

The golden door Emma Lazarus had lauded slammed shut.

From McCarthyism to the "HIV Ban"

In the 1950s, anxiety gripped American society over the sudden suspicion of homosexuals in its midst—and the sexual hysteria moved in tandem with a new "red scare." Homosexuals were seen as susceptible to blackmail, easy to enlist in treason. Moreover, to the McCarthyite mind, they shared with Communists the qualities of being gregarious yet secretive, concealing their true selves and loyalties, creating coteries and collectives that evaded surveillance. Republican Senate leader Kenneth Wherry said, "You can't hardly separate homosexuals from subversives. … A man of low morality is a menace in the government, and they are all tied up together."[48]

The panic prompted a campaign to drive homosexuals out of government service, as well as burgeoning and sometimes brutal FBI and police witch-hunts against ordinary people.[49] And it saw lesbian and gay immigrants banned from the U.S. by law. The bar dates from the 1952 Immigration and Nationality Act (INA), pushed through by Senator Pat McCarran of Nevada, a livid anti-Communist crusader.

The bill still stands as the basis for U.S. immigration policy—which it sweepingly revised. Slightly distancing itself from the whites-only past, it reinstated a trickle of Asian immigrants for the first time since 1924 (partly to improve the U.S.'s image as the Cold War militarized the Pacific); but it held to a lopsided bias for northern European groups.

---

[46] U.S. Bureau of the Census, *Historical Statistics of the United States, Colonial Times to 1957* (Washington, D.C.: Bureau of the Census, 1960), p. 56.

[47] John B. Trevor, quoted in Higham, *Strangers in the Land,* p. 324.

[48] Max Lerner, "The Senator and the Purge," *New York Post*, July 17, 1950, quoted in Jonathan Katz, *Gay American History: Lesbians and Gay Men in the U.S.A.* (New York: Harper Colophon, 1976), pp. 95.

[49] See David K. Johnson, *The Lavender Scare: The Cold War Persecution of Gays and Lesbians in the Federal Government* (Chicago: University of Chicago Press, 2004), as well as John D'Emilio, *Sexual Politics, Sexual Communities: The Making of a Homosexual Minority in the United States, 1940-1970* (Chicago: University of Chicago Press, 1983), pp. 38-56. D'Emilio in particular suggests that the "lavender scare," like the anti-immigrant panics of earlier years, was connected to fears of changing gender roles and family structure, particularly after the shifts of the war years: "Because the war removed large numbers of men and women from familial—and familiar—environments, it freed homosexual eroticism from some of the structural restraints that made it appear marginal and isolated" (p. 38).

By building into national quotas favorable treatment for immigrants with special skills, and for relatives of people already in the U.S., it laid the groundwork for the employment-based and family-sponsored preference categories of today.[50]

However, the act also allowed the government to ban people from the country on ideological grounds.[51] Moreover, it barred "aliens afflicted with *psychopathic personality*, epilepsy or *mental defect*."[52] Congress made clear that this was meant to exclude "homosexuals and sex perverts," even seeking an opinion from the U.S. Public Health Service that the term was broad enough to do so.[53] In 1965, the INA was amended, with new language prohibiting the entry of persons "afflicted with … *sexual deviation*."[54] With slight variations in the phrasing, for almost forty years the U.S. banned lesbians and gays from entering the country.

---

[50] Alicia J. Campi, Ph.D., "The McCarran-Walter Act: A Contradictory Legacy on Race, Quotas, and Ideology," immigration policy brief by the American Immigration Law Foundation, at http://www.ailf.org/ipc/policy_reports_2004_mccarranwalter.asp (retrieved December 26, 2005). See chapter III below for an explanation of these categories.

[51] President Truman vetoed the bill, calling it "neither a fitting instrument for our foreign policy nor a true reflection of what we stand for, at home and abroad, " but Congress easily overrode him. See Michael Ybarra, *Washington Gone Crazy: Senator Pat McCarran and the Great American Communist Hunt* (New York: Steerforth, 2004).

[52] Immigration and Nationality Act, § 212(a)(4), 66 Stat. at 182, emphasis added.

[53] The Senate Judiciary Committee had recommended in 1950 that " the classes of mentally defectives" barred from entry in existing legislation "should be enlarged to include homosexuals and other sex perverts" (S. Rep. No. 1515, 81st Cong., 2d Sess., p. 345). The proposed Immigration and Nationality Act thus originally contained an additional phrase expressly providing for the exclusion of aliens "who are homosexuals or sex perverts." These words were omitted from the law as passed, because—as the Senate Judiciary Committee explained—"The Public Health Service has advised that the provision for the exclusion of aliens afflicted with psychopathic personality or a mental defect … is sufficiently broad to provide for the exclusion of homosexuals and sex perverts. This change of nomenclature is not to be construed in any way as modifying the intent to exclude all aliens who are sexual deviates" (S. Rep. No. 1137, 82d Cong., 2d Sess., p. 9). See *Boutilier v Immigration Service,* Supreme Court of the United States, 387 U.S. 118 (1967).

[54] 1965 Amendments, Pub. L. No. 89-236, 79 Stat. 911 (1965), emphasis added. The 1965 legislation represented another broad restructuring of immigration. It finally abolished the 1924 Act's national quotas: with the civil rights movement combating racism at home, discriminating by national origin no longer seemed compatible with the U.S.'s expressed values.

Lesbian and Gay Immigrants in the Courts: A Summary

Despite right-wing claims that "judicial activism" favors lesbian, gay, bisexual, and transgender people, the immigration rights of LGBT people were consistently given scant support in jurisprudence from the 1950s to the 1980s. However, *Hill v INS* in 1983 effectively took the teeth out of the Immigration and Nationality Act's exclusion of lesbian and gay people from the US—and pointed toward the emerging protections for LGBT people's rights in more recent, non-immigration-related jurisprudence.

Boutilier v Immigration Service, 1967

In this case the Supreme Court decided whether lesbian and gay people were covered by the definition of "psychopathic personality." Twenty-one year old Clive Boutilier, a Canadian, had moved to the US in 1955 to join his mother, stepfather, and three siblings who already lived there. In 1963, he applied for U.S. citizenship, admitting that he had been arrested for sodomy in 1959. He was ordered deported.[55]

The case eventually reached the Supreme Court, which, in a 6-3 decision, upheld his deportation. The majority found that "Congress was not laying down a clinical test, but an exclusionary standard which it declared to be inclusive of those having homosexual and perverted characteristics ... Congress used the phrase 'psychopathic personality' not in the clinical sense, but to effectuate its purpose to exclude from entry all homosexuals and other sex perverts."[56] Dissenting, Justice William Douglas observed, "The term 'psychopathic personality' is a treacherous one like 'communist' or in an earlier day 'Bolshevik.' A label of this kind when freely used may mean only an unpopular person."[57]

Boutilier was torn from his partner of eight years. According to one historian, "Presumably distraught about the Court's decision ... Boutilier attempted suicide before leaving New York, survived a month-long coma that left him brain-damaged with permanent disabilities, and moved to southern Ontario with his parents, who took on the task of caring for him for more than twenty years." He died in Canada on April 12, 2003, only weeks before that country at last moved to legalize same-sex marriage.[58]

---

[55] Chris Duenas, "Coming to America: The Immigration Obstacle Facing Binational Same-Sex Couples," *Southern California Law Review,* vol. 73 (2000), pp. 811–841.

[56] *Boutilier v. Immigration Service,* Supreme Court of the United States, 387 U.S.118.

[57] Ibid.

[58] Mark Stein, "Forgetting and Remembering a Deported Alien," *History News Network*, November 3, 2003, http://hnn.us/articles/1769.html (retrieved December 26, 2005).

Adams v Howerton, 1980

Richard Adams, a U.S. citizen, lived in Colorado with his partner Anthony Sullivan, an Australian national. When Sullivan's visitor's visa expired, they persuaded their local county clerk to issue them a marriage license. Adams then asked the INS to classify Sullivan as his spouse for immigration purposes.[59]

The INS refused to acknowledge a relationship between "faggots"—as told above. The case eventually reached the Ninth Circuit Court of Appeals. The Court addressed two issues: whether for the purposes of immigration, a U.S. citizen's spouse must be a person of the opposite sex, and, if so, whether such limitation is constitutional.

The court concluded that Congress had intended to restrict the term "spouse" to opposite-sex married couples. The court then found that it was within Congress's plenary power thus to limit access to immigration benefits, stating that the Supreme Court "has upheld the broad power of Congress to determine immigration policy in the face of challenges" based on constitutional claims.[60] The Supreme Court refused to hear an appeal.

Hill v INS, 1983

On August 2, 1979, the Surgeon General issued a new policy stating that the U.S. Public Health Service should no longer consider "homosexuality per se to be a 'mental disease or defect,'" citing "current and generally accepted canons of medical practice with respect to homosexuality."[61] Since the exclusion of homosexuals was based on the Public Health Service's findings, this created problems for the Immigration and Naturalization Service. In response, in 1980 the INS issued its own "Guidelines and Procedures for Inspection of Aliens Who Are Suspected of Being Homosexual." Non-citizens would no longer be asked about their sexual orientation, but if one admitted to being gay or the fact was revealed during inspection, the INS would not need medical certification. The admission could be used to deport him or her.

In 1980, Carl Hill, a British citizen, arrived at San Francisco International Airport and told immigration authorities he was gay. His resulting exclusion led to a court case that came before the Ninth Circuit Court in 1983. The court decided that non-citizens could not be shut out of the country based solely on their own admission to homosexuality. The law required Public Health Service certification, and the INS could not circumvent this through its own, different guidelines.[62]

---

[59] Duenas, p. 80.

[60] *Adams v. Howerton,* Ninth Circuit, 673 F.2d 1038 (1980).

[61] Board of Immigration Appeal, No. A-2420404969, *Matter of Hill*, quoted from opinion.

[62] *Hill v. INS,* Ninth Circuit, 714 F.2d at 1472 (1983).

The decision indicated that future denials of entry to homosexuals would face serious legal scrutiny. However, not until the Immigration Act of 1990 was the issue finally settled: Congress decided that lesbians and gays could no longer be excluded based on their sexual orientation.

The ideological provisions of McCarran's immigration act finally were repealed in 1990—after denying entry over the years to such figures as Yves Montand, Gabriel Garcia Marquez, and Pierre Trudeau. The same 1990 reform also eliminated the bar against homosexuals and the references to "psychopathic personality or mental defect." [63] The change in immigration law came late.[64] The U.S. was the last industrialized country to cling to a complete ban on homosexuals' entry.

The 1990 Immigration Act also quietly authorized the Department of Health and Human Services to remove a ban, in effect since 1987, on the entry of foreign nationals with HIV. When the Clinton administration tried to do so three years later, however, a thunderous backlash ensued—much of it following nineteenth-century channels, identifying immigrants with disease and closed borders with immunity and health. In 1993, Congress wrote the ban back into law, specifying that excludable conditions "include infection with the etiologic agent for acquired immune deficiency syndrome."

One observer writes that "The U.S. Immigration and Naturalization Service currently conducts the largest mandatory HIV-testing program in the world. Every applicant for permanent residence over the age of fifteen is required to undergo HIV testing, and largely without informed consent or pre-and post-testing."[65] Applicants for non-immigrant entry are questioned on their HIV status, and if they admit to being positive, can be refused admission.[66] If the government suspects them of HIV infection, it can require an HIV test; people entering the U.S. with HIV medications in their luggage can be questioned or expelled. Non-immigrants who are HIV-positive can request (and can be denied) a waiver for short trips under limited conditions. U.S. policy on HIV and travel has been called "one of the most unenlightened in the world."[67]

---

[63] Robert Foss, "The Demise of the Homosexual Exclusion: New Possibilities for Gay and Lesbian Immigration," *Harvard Civil Rights-Civil Liberties Law Review*, vol. 29 (1994), pp. 439-446.

[64] The American Psychological Association had removed homosexuality from its roster of psychiatric disorders in 1973.

[65] Alana Klein, "HIV/AIDS and Immigration: Final Report," Canadian HIV/AIDS Legal Network, 2001, p. 27.

[66] The language of affliction clearly recalls the ban on people "afflicted with … sexual deviation."

[67] William B. Rubenstein, Ruth Eisenberg and Lawrence O. Gostin. *The Authoritative ACLU Guide to the Rights of People Living with HIV Disease and AIDS* (Carbondale: Southern Illinois University, 1996), p. 315. The biannual International AIDS Conference, the most important gathering of experts and activists combating the

The United Nations International Guidelines on HIV/AIDS and Human Rights note that "There is no public health rationale for restricting liberty of movement or choice of residence on the grounds of HIV status."[68] Two experts observe:

> HIV is well-established everywhere in the world, and attempts to halt its spread by controlling the movement of infected or potentially infected persons have proven futile and expensive besides causing considerable hardship.[69]

Preserving the myth that HIV/AIDS is a threat external to the U.S.'s borders, the ban encourages a false sense of safety, damaging public health rather than defending it. It feeds on, and further feeds, archaic associations between immigration and contamination, the alien and the unclean. Finally, the ban exposes lesbian, gay, bisexual, and transgender immigrants and visitors to particular harassment, given stereotypes which associate them with HIV infection. The fears that locked the "golden door," and defined deserving immigrants as "mentally defective," still run strong.

Defended from What?

On September 10, 1996, by a huge margin, the Senate approved the "Defense of Marriage Act" (DOMA). Passed in haste, and signed in an almost furtive late-night ceremony by President Clinton ten days later, the measure was an election-year reaction to the possibility that Hawaii might become the first state to recognize equality in civil marriage. (Seven years later, Massachusetts did.)

The bill did two things. It declared that no state was obliged to recognize "a relationship between persons of the same sex that is treated as marriage" by any other state or jurisdiction. And it defined marriage, for all purposes of the federal government, as

---

disease, is no longer held in the U.S. because of the ban. The WHO has a policy of not sponsoring international meetings to discuss AIDS in countries with HIV/AIDS-specific short-term travel restrictions. See World Health Organization. "WHO policy of non-sponsorship of international conferences on AIDS in countries with HIV/AIDS-specific short term travel restrictions," February 1993, with reference to World Health Assembly Resolution WHA41.24 (1988) ("Avoidance of discrimination in relation to HIV-infected people and people with AIDS").

[68] Office of the United Nations High Commissioner for Human Rights and the Joint United Nations Programme on HIV/AIDS, "HIV/AIDS and Human Rights-International Guidelines (from the second international consultation on HIV/AIDS and human rights, 23-25 September 1996, Geneva)," U.N. Doc. HR/PUB/98/1, Geneva, 1998.

[69] Josef Decosas and Alix Adrien, quoted in Klein, p. 51.

"only a legal union between one man and one woman as husband and wife." The word "spouse" now refers "only to a person of the opposite sex who is a husband or wife."[70]

This foreclosed the possibility that foreign, permanent same-sex partners of U.S. citizens could be recognized as "spouses" under current U.S. immigration law.

The constitutionality of DOMA remains uncertain.[71] As a panicked reaction to the mere prospect of a state recognizing same-sex relationships, however, it was telling—and foretelling. Since then, nineteen states have approved constitutional amendments barring equality in civil marriage.[72] Some prohibited giving *any* legal status to relationships other than heterosexual marriage. The results are devastating. Ohio's draconian amendment, for instance, forced a judge in 2005 to void part of the state's domestic violence law. He threw out a felony charge against a man accused of abusing his unmarried *heterosexual* partner—because the state constitution now barred any law or ruling that would "create or recognize a legal status for relationships of unmarried individuals."[73]

Amid the furor, President Bush in 2004 endorsed a national constitutional amendment banning equality in marriage. Many want this to go further, and, like Ohio's, to bar civil unions and all forms of recognizing unmarried relationships, anywhere in policy or law.[74]

Lesbian, gay, bisexual, and transgender people's relationships are thus central, not collateral casualties in a raging culture war. The moral panic reaches beyond them. "Gay marriage" is a wedge issue, wielded to restrict other forms of personal autonomy. Most

---

[70] Defense of Marriage Act, Pub. L. No. 104-199, 100 Stat. 2419 (Sept. 21, 1996), codified at 1 U.S.C. § 7 and 28 U.S.C. § 1738C.

[71] Article 4, section 1 of the United States Constitution states that "Full Faith and Credit shall be given in each State to the public Acts, Records, and judicial Proceedings of every other State," and that "Congress may by general Laws prescribe the Manner in which such Acts, Records, and Proceedings shall be proved and the Effect thereof." In a range of decisions, the Supreme Court has not fully clarified the extent to which a state can decline "full faith and credit" on the grounds of its own strong public policy, or the extent to which Congress' permitted regulation of "the effect thereof" includes the ability to retract it. See Paige Chabora, "Congress' Power Under the Full Faith and Credit Clause and the Defense of Marriage Act of 1996," *Nebraska Law Review*, vol. 76 (1997), and Julie L. B. Johnson, "The Meaning of 'General Laws': The Extent of Congress's Power Under the Full Faith and Credit Clause and the Constitutionality of the Defense of Marriage Act," *University of Pennsylvania Law Review,* vol. 145 (1997).

[72] This includes amendments in Louisiana and Nebraska which have been overturned and are still subject to litigation.

[73] "Judge: Domestic violence law for marrieds only—Backlash from anti-gay marriage amendment," Associated Press, March 24, 2005.

[74] See Michael Farris, "Critical Decision on Text of Constitutional Amendment Protecting Marriage," February 5, 2004, at http://www.cwfa.org/articles/5208/CWA/family/ (retrieved January 2, 2005).

of the groups in the trenches opposing it also fight to eliminate abortion, and many support laws restricting divorce.[75] Nearly all agitate for curbs on legal immigration.

Striking in this culture war is the cultural defensiveness: the notion that people who want to enjoy the dignity and benefits of marriage seek to destroy it, or that people who admire the United States and want to enter its borders are inevitably its invading enemies. The rhetoric of invisible foes, values endangered, redoubts taken, battles lost, is heard everywhere. It mimics the pessimism of a Francis Walker or a Madison Grant, men who saw lifeways beleaguered by difference.

Indeed, many anti-immigrant activists sound like time-capsule transmissions from the 1880s or the 1920s, with minor changes. *Then,* the aliens who menaced "American values" were largely Slavs, Jews, Italians; *now* those groups are seen as safely assimilated, and the enemy Other has grown darker and more distant. But the stereotypes, the fears of sterility and decline, are the same. [76]

When lesbian, gay, bisexual, and transgender people's rights involve the country's borders, then, the response will likely be furious. One conservative warned that the Uniting American Families Act "would make the United States a magnet for homosexuals to come to our shores."[77] When a Texas congressman supported the Act, opponents charged him with "allowing homosexuals … a free pass to bypass our immigration laws by bringing over anyone they say is their 'partner'"—people "who will

---

[75] Bridget E. Maher, "Why Marriage Should be Privileged In Public Policy," Family Research Council, at http://www.frc.org/index.cfm?i=IS03D1&f=WU03J07 (retrieved December 15, 2004). See also "Anti-Gay Groups Active in Massachusetts: A Closer Look," National Gay and Lesbian Task Force, at http://www.TheTaskForce.org/marriagecenter (retrieved November 11, 2004). The same paper points out that the website of Concerned Women for America, a powerful conservative group that describes itself as a "public policy women's organization," "had 602 documents on its website that contained the word 'homosexual,' but only 97 referring to 'health care,' 80 with the word 'poverty' … and six containing 'child support.'" Only seventy-one documents referred to "rape," nineteen to "domestic violence," and none at all to "pay equity." Ibid., p 15.

[76] David H. Bennett, *Party of Fear: From Nativist Movements to the New Right in American History* (New York: Knopf, 1995) argues for direct continuity between nineteenth-century racism and xenophobia and contemporary anti-immigrant and fundamentalist movements. In the present day, Pat Buchanan blames U.S. "decline" on immigrants: "America is ceasing to be one country." But gender and sexuality propel population shifts. The problem, he says, is Western women: "We know how they are not having children—birth control or abortion or sterilization or whatever. But the reasons why are the economy and culture and feminism, and the women are doing what they want to do. I don't know how politically, in a democratic society … we can force changes upon women and upon men as well. But I do have some ideas …" "How the West was lost: Pat Buchanan discusses his new book with Geoff Metcalf," *World Net Daily*, December 23, 2001, at http://www.worldnetdaily.com/news/article.asp?ARTICLE_ID=25797 (retrieved January 4, 2003).

[77] Robert Knight, director of the Culture and Family Institute of Concerned Women for America, quoted in Jeff Johnson, "Congressman Promotes Immigration Privileges for Homosexuals," *Christian News Service,* at http://www.cnsnews.com/ViewPrint.asp?Page=%5CPolitics%5Carchive%5C200209%5CPOL20020923d.html (retrieved October 31, 2004).

not only take American jobs but also worsen the AIDS epidemic (including free health care once they get here)."[78]

In the wake of the September 11 attacks—much as in the 1920s—anxiety over terrorism has twisted all immigration debates. The 2001 Patriot Act revived forms of ideological exclusion. Anti-terrorist rhetoric insinuates itself into arguments over sexual rights as well. When the Supreme Court struck down sodomy laws in 2003, Lou Sheldon, a right-wing activist, said, "This is a 9/11, major wake-up call that the enemy is at our doorsteps."[79] When border officials halted a Canadian same-sex married couple because they tried to use the same customs form—like any other spouses—the conservative group Concerned Women for America declared:

> Many have feared that lax border security would allow terrorists to easily enter the United States from Canada. However, U.S. Customs officials at Pearson International Airport in Toronto were able to stop the latest pair of "domestic terrorists."[80]

What threat did that family represent? And what needs to be defended?

---

[78] Tom Owens, "Why Rep. Nick Lampson is 'Bought and Paid For' by the Homosexual Lobby," at http://www.liberallampson.com, and "The Shocking Truth about Nick Lampson's Connections to the Homosexual Lobby," mailing distributed to voters, at http://www.liberallampson.com/lampsonmailer.pdf (retrieved November 25, 2005). The UAFA in no way offers "free health care" or any other benefit save immigration recognition.

[79] Quoted in Robert B. Bluey, "Court's Ruling on Sodomy Fuels Fight for Same-Sex Marriage," *Christian News Service,* June 27, 2003, at http://www.newsmax.com/archives/articles/2003/6/27/120250.shtml (retrieved June 28, 2003).

[80] James Kimball, "Homosexuals Pose New Threat to U.S. Border Security," press release from Concerned Women for America, September 24, 2003, at http://www.csfa.com/printerfriendly.asp?id=4629&department+cwa&categoryid=family (retrieved September 25, 2003).

III. Closed Doors: U.S. Visas and Immigration

This chapter gives basic facts about the visa and immigration system and how lesbian, gay, bisexual, and transgender people fit into it—or do not.

Most U.S. citizens know nothing about what foreign nationals face to enter or stay in the United States. "People don't realize the implications" of the immigration process, says Nathalie Fuz, a French national living in New York with her U.S. partner Kelly McGowan. Nathalie, who owns two retail stores in the city, is able to stay, temporarily, on an employment visa. However, she says, "Unless they're within a binational relationship, nobody understands it. Not just the mainstream, but within our community"—the lesbian, gay, bisexual, and transgender community. "Yet daily incidents remind you that you don't have rights, not only as someone gay, but as a binational couple."[81]

Yet, says Barbara, who lives in Massachusetts with her U.K. partner Susan, "When it's your life, you're researching it constantly, researching always, because it's very hard to keep up with all of the current information." [82] Rafael Jaen, a Venezuelan and an internationally known costume designer, has an O-1 (outstanding ability) visa letting him stay in the U.S. with his partner of ten years, Stephen Brady. He says, "My whole life is organized around my visa status and everything I need to do to keep the visa."[83]

The unequal treatment of lesbian and gay partnerships is only one among many interlinked inequities riddling the immigration system. Marta Donayre, co-founder of Love Sees No Borders, a group for binational gay and lesbian couples, points out:

> Women have a harder time coming to the country. To get a tourist visa, you have to prove that you have ties back home. Women are less likely to have bank accounts or own property, so it is harder for them to qualify. Third World status makes it far more difficult as well—which is

---

[81] Human Rights Watch/Immigration Equality interview with Nathalie Fuz and Kelly McGowan, New York, October 14, 2005.

[82] Human Rights Watch/Immigration Equality telephone interview with Barbara and Susan (last names withheld at their request), October 11, 2005.

[83] Human Rights Watch/Immigration Equality interview with Rafael Jaen and Stephen Brady, New York, March 25, 2005.

about race and also is about economics: so in immigration policy, you clearly see the intersection of race, gender and class at work.[84]

Leslie Bulbuk and Marta Donayre, 2006 © 2006 Private

The system is both extremely complex and pitched towards the estrangement of couples. We ask readers to try an experiment in the ensuing pages. Whoever you may be, imagine this: you are a U.S. citizen who, traveling abroad, has met someone—the love of your life. You share dreams and ambitions—and the same sex. What you don't share is citizenship; he or she is not from the United States. You have gone home after a period together overseas; but the two of you plan to be reunited, as soon as your partner can join you in the U.S.

This may actually *be* your story, in which case the coming pages may ring true. If it is not, you may learn some unexpected facts.

[84] Human Rights Watch/Immigration Equality interview with Marta Donayre and Leslie Bulbuk, Oakland, November 11, 2005.

Exploring Immigrant Visas

We Are (Not) Family

Immigrant visas offer foreigners permanent residence in the U.S.—obviously your first choice, since the two of you want to be lastingly together. Most immigrant visas are either *family-based* or *employment-based*; in either case, a U.S. family member or possible employer must file a petition on your partner's behalf. If U.S. Citizenship and Immigration Services (the agency which used to be called the Immigration and Naturalization Service) approves it, your partner will have to apply for *lawful permanent residency*. A lawful permanent resident (LPR) receives a card giving the right to live and work in the U.S. permanently (called the "green card" because it used to be printed on green paper).

Here is the first problem. "Family reunification" lies at the heart of the U.S. immigration system. U.S. citizens can sponsor family members—parents, spouses, children or siblings—for permanent immigration. About two-thirds of all immigrant visas are family-based. During a recent debate on immigration reform, one Republican congressman declared, "Prolonging the separation of spouses from each other … is inconsistent with the principles on which this nation was founded."[85]

The family reunification system is flawed—limited in reach and plagued by backlogs which suspend some family members (especially sisters and brothers) in indefinite delay. For you, though, it is irrelevant. Your partnership—your family—does not count at all. Current U.S. law, particularly the Defense of Marriage Act, forbids recognizing same-sex permanent partners as "spouses" or family members for immigration purposes. The "heart of the system" suddenly seems heartless.

The denial is particularly galling when you learn about what is called a "fiancé(e) visa."[86] The K-1 visa allows the intended spouse of a U.S. citizen to enter the U.S. for ninety days, to marry him or her and then apply for permanent residence. The U.S. citizen must simply show that he and his (or her) partner:

- have met in person at least once in the last two years (exceptions are possible),
- have a *bona fide* intention to marry, and

---

[85] Rep. Raymond McGrath, quoted in Chris Duenas, "Coming to America: The Immigration Obstacle Facing Binational Same-Sex Couples," *Southern California Law Review*, vol. 73 (2000), pp. 811–841.

[86] This type of visa is sometimes called a "hybrid visa." Strictly speaking there is no "hybrid" category; however, the term has come to be used for these visas because they allow short-term non-immigrant entry, but quick conversion to immigrant status.

- are "legally able and actually willing to conclude a valid marriage in the United States" within ninety days after the partner gets there.[87]

Obviously, lesbian and gay couples are not eligible for K visas because of the "valid marriage" criterion. Even if they have a "bona fide intention to marry," their marriage will not be recognized by U.S. law. You also realize the only requirement imposed on opposite-sex couples in your situation is that they *intend* to marry and have met *once* in person. You and your lover might have lived together for decades, or even married in countries where it is legal; it would make no difference.

Employment-Based Immigrant Visas

The other option for your partner is immigrating to the United States to work. This requires sponsorship by an employer in the U.S. For nearly all employment-based immigrant visas, the employer has to show the government that there are no qualified U.S. workers to fill the position.

You begin looking for companies willing to sponsor your partner for an immigrant visa. No luck. Employment-based immigrant visas are very hard to get: all the types have strict limits on the number annually available, and all have rigorous qualifications. (For example, one category is for people who invest $1,000,000 in a new U.S. business.) It would demand perseverance and high standards of proof, not just on your partner's part but on the employer's. Few companies can afford the time and effort.

Relationship Roulette: The Diversity Lottery

The 1990 immigration reforms which finally struck the ban on lesbians and gays entering the U.S. also created the "visa lottery." "Family reunification" means that a few countries whose nationals are already heavily represented in the U.S. may crowd most other countries out of access to immigration. To compensate, places in the visa lottery are reserved for applicants from the underrepresented nations. It is often called the "diversity lottery."

Many countries are not eligible for the visa lottery, and the number of slots is limited by law—to 55,000, against millions who apply. Depending on where your partner lives, you

---

[87] Immigration and Nationality Act, sections 101(a)(15)(k) and 214(d). In addition, the K-2 visa allows entry to the dependent minor children of a fiancé. In 2000, the Legal Immigration and Family Equity Act (the LIFE Act) also extended K visa benefits to the spouses of U.S. citizens, and their unmarried children under age 21, who are outside the U.S. and awaiting the processing of their green card petitions.

may be able to place your hopes in the lottery as a last-ditch chance—but you are submitting your shared future to the throw of the dice.

Non-Immigrant Visas

This leaves you with an uncomfortable decision: to surrender the hope of permanence and find a temporary way for your partner to enter the country, so you can be together, if uncertainly, for a time. This means investigating the non-immigrant visa options, which do not offer a path to permanent, legalized status. They are of two main kinds: a) *non-employment-based, non-immigrant* visas; b) *employment-based* visas.

Single and Suspect, Coupled and Complicit

The most obvious option is the *visitor's* visa—in technical terms, the B-1/B-2 visa. The B-1 lets people enter the U.S. for up to six months for business, such as consulting with clients, meeting with business associates, or attending professional, scientific, or religious conventions. B-1 visitors cannot get a salary from a U.S. employer. The B-2 visa is similar, but is for "pleasure" travel. B-2 visas allow a stay of up to six months for reasons such as tourism, visiting friends or relatives, rest, or medical treatment. B-1/2 visas also do not let the holder work.[88] Other non-immigrant visas that also do not include work authorization are F-1 or student visas and J-1 or training visas.

---

[88] In discussing B visas, it is important to note that in one relatively minor way, U.S. immigration policy does recognize same-sex partners—though without any benefit to binational couples. A foreign national who comes to the United States on a long-term non-immigrant visa is eligible to bring his or her foreign "cohabiting partner" on a B-2, or visitor's, visa. This policy was set out in a ruling by the INS in 1993. It was formalized by the State Department in 2001, in a cable stating: "B-2 classification is appropriate for cohabitating partners of long term non-immigrants ... The [Foreign Affairs Manual] is being advised to expressly incorporate this...interpretation." (Document R 091817Z Jul 01, Cable from SecState WashDC to All Diplomatic and Consular Posts, UNCLAS State 118790.)

It is not clear that lesbian and gay partners were originally meant to benefit from this policy. Other eligible individuals include "extended family members and other household members not eligible for derivative status" (ibid.): it is reasonably clear that the INS mainly meant to make it easier for foreign workers on long-term visas (such as well-paid executives) to bring domestic help as well as non-dependent relatives from home. "Derivative status," referred to above, is designed to maintain family unity for long-term non-immigrants. If an individual is approved for a long-term international employee visa, his or her different-sex spouse is eligible, along with their children, for derivative status. This confers the same immigration benefits on the family members as does the principal visa. Lesbian and gay permanent partners of long-term non-immigrants do not qualify for derivative status. The Foreign Affairs Manual states, "Unless the relationship is recognized under law as being fully equivalent in all respects to traditional legal marriage and grants the parties all the same rights and duties as a traditional marriage, the cohabitating partner cannot qualify for derivative status. However," the Manual continues, "such aliens may be classified as B-2 visitors, provided they are otherwise qualified for B classification. This is true for both opposite and same-sex partners." (9 U.S. Department of State, Foreign Affairs Manual, Notes to Sec. 40.1)

To lesbian and gay immigrants, it is a clear that the government is trying to have it both ways—denying recognition to their partnerships broadly, but permitting a small but convenient exception. Moreover, by carving

You carefully check that your partner will not be doing anything wrong in using a tourist visa to visit you. The Foreign Affairs Manual—the U.S. State Department's guidelines for all its employees, consular officers included— endorses such uses for the tourist visa, stating: "B-2 visas are appropriate for individuals traveling to the United States for tourism purposes, or to make social visits to relatives or friends."[89]

Still, there are particular burdens lesbian, gay, bisexual, and transgender people may face in the visa application process—and these leave you anything but confident.

To apply, your partner must ordinarily go to a local U.S. consulate.[90] The consular process can take time, and cost money. It may mean facing a consular officer in an interview—and handing over the fate of your relationship to his or her discretion.[91] Certain health conditions or a criminal record are grounds for rejection; so, too, is the suspicion of *immigrant intent*—which means a consular official, for any reason, thinks it likely your partner will not return home when the visit is over. In fact, your partner is guilty until proven innocent.[92] He or she must prove:

- strong enough "ties abroad" (that is, in the home country) to give a "strong inducement to return," such as a permanent job there, business interests, or close family members who remain at home;[93]
- enough funds to afford the visit, so that your partner will not need—or want—to take unlawful employment while in the U.S.

---

this loophole, the government shamefacedly shows it has no across-the-board, consistent rationale for categorically denying immigration rights to partners in same-sex relationships.

[89] 9 U.S. Department of State, *Foreign Affairs Manual*, Notes to 22 CFR Sec. 41.31.

[90] In 1986, the U.S. created a Visa Waiver Program for which twenty-seven countries (mostly European) are now eligible. The program allows nationals of these countries to visit the U.S. for tourism or business for ninety days without obtaining a visa—with the aim of "promoting better relations with U.S. allies ... stimulating the tourism industry, and permitting the Department of State to focus consular resources in other areas." ("Visa Waiver Program [VWP]", at http://travel.state.gov/visa/temp/without/without_1990.html, retrieved January 4, 2006.) Nations entering under the program are still subject to screening at the port of entry.

[91] One expert has written that "The B-2 visa category can be one of the most complex and difficult ... because the issues and factors involved in the decision are almost entirely subjective." Carl Falstrom, "The B-2 Visitor for Pleasure—The Most Issued Visa," *Immigration and Nationality Law Handbook, 2001-2 Edition*, American Immigration Lawyers Association (AILA). For several years, Representative Barney Frank (D-MA) has proposed legislation to create an appeals board for consular decisions.

[92] The law states: "Every alien...shall be presumed to be an immigrant until he established to the satisfaction of the consular officer, at the time of application for a visa, and the immigration officers, at the time of application for admission, that he is entitled to non-immigrant status": Immigration and Nationality Act § 214(b).

[93] Carl Falstrom, "The B-2 Visitor for Pleasure—The Most Issued Visa," *Immigration and Nationality Law Handbook, 2001-2 Edition*.

The first requirement is often hard for lesbians and gays. Suppose your partner is a gay man in his mid-twenties. The U.S. consulate will ask if he is married. If he were, his wife (assuming she did not plan to accompany him) would, in their eyes, give him reason to return—a sort of hostage to ensure he doesn't try to stay in the U.S. He does not have a wife, though. Without a legally recognized married relationship at home, gays and lesbians may appear to consular officials as insufficiently "rooted" to return.

The consular official may ask your partner why he is *not* married. (Officials can ask any question they want.) Should he say he is gay? Should he mention his U.S. partner? The very fact of having a relationship with a U.S. citizen works against lesbian and gay foreign nationals who try to visit. The official is likely to assume he is actually seeking to stay in the U.S. Frequently the very fact of being lesbian or gay is enough to arouse suspicion. And yet if your partner misrepresents himself in any part of the application process, that can also be reason to deny the visa.

Further, tourist visas, as well as student and training visas, bar receiving wages while in the U.S. Your partner must show enough money to pay her own way. However, the law allows visa applicants to show they have a *sponsor* instead: a U.S. citizen or permanent resident who promises financial backing during the stay. Unlike the sponsor for an immigrant visa, this need not be a family member. Thus, you can do this for your partner.

Yet, for many LGBT people trying to enter the U.S., this very act of sponsorship can raise suspicion and cause the visa to be denied. If consular officials suspect—whether rightly or wrongly—that the applicant is in a relationship with the sponsor, they may well assume he or she does not plan to return.[94]

[94] It is important to note that no visa in itself authorizes entry to the U.S. It simply indicates that the holder's application has been reviewed by a U.S. consular officer, and that the officer found him or her eligible to travel to the port of entry for a specific purpose. In other words, each entry to the United States for a foreign national is a two-step process—first, obtaining a visa (which allows getting on the plane but does not guarantee getting across the border), and, second, passing inspection at a U.S. port of entry. Anyone can be denied entry with a valid visa, even if they have always complied with the visa's terms—have never overstayed or worked illegally—if (for example) an immigration official believes he or she has been spending too much time in the United States.

Visa Denied

"I'm an American and I'm not totally free," began the e-mail Denis Symington sent us:

I'm not equal. I'm discriminated against. I'm looked down upon. I don't have my rights, my equality and liberty and justice and all those other things that many years ago were beaten into my head in the fourth grade by Sister Mary Honoria. The same words I was told make America such a special place in the world. They are denied to me by the U.S. government. They don't apply to me—I'm gay....

That was a tough morning outside the stone gates of the U.S. Embassy in Moscow. Disbelief, anger, frustration and tears consumed me as I sat there with the second Declined *on my life partner's passport. He was in shock. I was speechless. We sat in silence for ages.*

We met nine years ago in a park in front of the Bolshoi Theater, just yards from Red Square. A mutual friend introduced us and we began dating. I was working for a U.S. company at the time, living in Moscow. My partner, Abakar Zurayev, was a teacher of English in a local children's school. ... We traveled all over the world, seeing the sights and discovering more about each other. We even traveled to the U.S. a few times to visit my family. ... We even have a picture together in front of the Statue of Liberty. A fact that is enormously ironic. Give me your poor, your tired, your weary—blah, blah—just don't give me your self-supporting, committed, long-term, gay partners of nine years.

I transferred back to New Hampshire with my company; we secured a student visa for my partner Aba. We built a house, in Dover, New Hampshire. Aba was enrolled in a technical college, we were active in the community, we started saving for our future, a long life we had planned together. This was at the six-year point of our relationship.

Aba needed to renew his passport in Moscow and see his son and family. This required that his new passport have a new student visa so he could continue with the two remaining years of his surgical technology studies. Then it happened.

I got the phone call at 6 a.m. He could not breathe. ... Tears filled his words, then mine. I sat on the bathroom floor as I listened to him recount the previous few hours. Our life was so good till that point, committed and secure. Now it was held over a chasm of uncertainty and tough decisions.

The U.S. Embassy in Moscow decided his surgical technology program was not a reason to study in the US, and he should pursue this program in Russia. Denied. ... How could my government do this to me?

Denis flew to Moscow to be with Aba, and to help him appeal. They "were denied again by the same clerk, who wanted to hear nothing about us, our life together, our home. She just kept calling for the next person in line."

Eventually, the couple was able to resettle in the U.K. together. Denis writes that they wait for one thing—the passage of the UAFA:

I am so grateful to the British for this opportunity, but this is not home. Not a day goes by that I don't want to go home to my house in Dover, drive my car, spend weekends with my sister, see our friends. I log on every day reading Yahoo News, expecting to see by some miracle this bill was passed and I can walk down to the U.S. embassy in London with Aba and get his green card. We can move back to my homeland—move into our house—work and get on with our lives. One day it will come. But when?

(From an email to Immigration Equality from Denis Symington, August 2003; in a slightly different form Denis published his story as "Kicked Out of America," *The Advocate*, February 4, 2004.)

Employment-Based Non-Immigrant Visas

Instead of a visitor's visa, you and your partner may decide to explore *employer-sponsored non-immigrant visas.* These allow your partner to take a job in the U.S. with a U.S.-based company.[95] They are not a path to permanent residence (unlike the employment-based immigrant visas). But just because of that, you assume they should be simpler to get than immigrant visas.

In fact they are hard to obtain—for anyone, straight or gay. The H1B, the most common work-based visa, requires verifying the applicant's relevant special skills as well as education or background in the area of employment. If your partner has a college degree in sociology, she will be ineligible for an H1B if her proposed job is not directly related to that field. This (and the cost of filing an application) shuts out many.

There is yet another problem. If your partner actually is able to enter on a work visa, she can stay only so long as she keeps her job. This makes it easy for employers to exploit foreign partners in binational couples. Across the board and across the country, innumerable immigrants suffer severe abuses at work. Yet, for people who face workplace harassment or discrimination—because they are lesbian, gay, bisexual or transgender or for any other reason—but are doubly discouraged from reporting it because their relationship as well as visa depends on their employment, the disempowerment may be overwhelming.

However, the real difficulty you have with all the non-immigrant visas—tourist or work-based—is precisely their salient characteristic. They expire. None of them offers your relationship the permanence heterosexual couples can take for granted.

The longer they last, the greater the disruption and heartbreak when the time runs out. Student visas can last the length of a college or graduate education, employment-based non-immigrant visas for three or six years. If your partner has been lucky enough to get such a visa, you have likely built a life together in your new community. You may have bought a home or had children, all while looking to a common future. Yet, the longing to create intertwined lives may actually damage your chances to stay together. People on visitors', student, or training visas must maintain non-immigrant intent. If immigration officials find out you have a permanent relationship in the U.S., that can be taken as intent to stay. Bad luck or an unwitting mistake may mean that your shared happiness leads to your deportation.

---

[95] Examples include the H1B visa and the E visa. An H1B visa is available to "specialty occupation workers," such as fashion models or professionals who need a license for their work. An E-1 visa is for people involved in substantial business trade between the U.S. and their country. E-2 visas are available for people who have invested substantial money in a business they direct in the U.S

Life on an H1B Visa

Robert, a U.S. citizen, and his partner Adam, who is Canadian, had been together for twelve years when they wrote to us. For six of those years, Adam had been able to stay in the U.S. on a student visa while studying music. At the end of that time, Robert says, "We exhausted student visa options." Adam, however, is one of the comparatively lucky ones: he managed to get an H1B work visa as music director for a local church.

Not only did this visa cost us $12,000 in legal fees to obtain, we spent two agonizing years of worry and despair waiting for the INS to adjudicate the case, due to major bureaucratic bungling on the agency's part. H1B has a maximum length of six years, and must be renewed after just three. We are currently beginning the renewal process, and hoping for the best, but at the end of the six years, Adam is legally required to leave the United States for a period of not less than one year. What kind of life can we build together, with so little hope of stability, and no real security?

For four years now, they have lived in the small New England town where Adam works. Adam is an accomplished harpsichordist and organist and a respected scholar of early music. But, Robert explains,

Competition for teaching positions is fierce. Adam's non-resident status puts him at a distinct disadvantage ... because every prospective employer must obtain a separate visa if they wish to hire him. As for his performance career, he is required to obtain a special visa for each and every paid gig, and this visa can only be obtained at a border station. The absurd situation of having to travel five hundred miles round-trip to the Canadian border station, in order to play a $300 gig right here in our town, leaves two choices: non-compliance accompanied by worry and guilt, or no gigs at all. Due to this lack of parity with his peers, Adam's professional development is severely restricted and stunted.

Robert adds,

> *I am a United States citizen and yet am denied the basic right to sponsor my immigrant partner for U.S. residency. This is clear and blatant discrimination. Our small town is a patriotic town, due in part to its claim of hosting the longest running Independence Day parade in the country. On the Fourth of July, the climax of the calendar year here, when that parade comes down the street, how do you think I feel? I love my country, yet the revelry of the crowd rings empty for me, because it celebrates, in part, that fundamental freedom, the pursuit of happiness. Current immigration law excludes me, in a very real way, from that pursuit.*
>
> From an e-mail to Immigration Equality from Robert and Adam (names changed at their request), August 22, 2003.

Asylum

It may be that in your partner's home country, lesbian, gay, bisexual, and transgender people face imprisonment or even death.

For over a decade, U.S. policy has offered asylum to people who, in their own lands, are persecuted—their safety or freedom threatened—because of their sexual orientation.[96] There have also been some (though fewer) cases granting asylum based on gender identity, as well as cases granting asylum based on HIV status. If your partner comes from a country where persecution of lesbian, gay, bisexual, and transgender people is regular and real, he or she may choose to claim asylum in the U.S.—not as a pretext to remain in your relationship, but in order to stay alive and free.

Amid growing anti-immigrant pressure, gaining asylum has become harder for everyone. However, certain factors particularly affect people making claims based on their sexual orientation or gender identity. Under a 1996 law that tightened access to asylum, applicants have only one year after their arrival to file. The fact that sexual orientation is protected in U.S. asylum policy is not well-known; some LGBT people do not hear about the possibility in time. Some others are afraid to press a claim because of homophobia and possible violence in their own immigrant communities here.

---

[96] In 1989 Fidel Armand Toboso-Alfonso, a Cuban citizen, claimed refugee status in the United States because, as a homosexual, he was persecuted at home. He was granted withholding of deportation, and the Board of Immigration Appeals (BIA) upheld the decision in 1990. In 1994, then Attorney General Janet Reno ruled that this case be considered a precedent, meaning that asylum officers, immigration judges, and the BIA had to accept its example in the future.

Some asylum officers and immigration judges do not fully grasp issues of sexuality or gender identity. They may treat your partner with sarcasm or contempt. They may tell him or her simply to "keep it secret" at home and be safe—failing to see that concealing a crucial part of one's self, like hiding a religious belief, is itself a form of persecution. In places where repression of LGBT people is severe, their networks and communities often have been driven underground. Getting information to support your asylum claim may be insuperably hard.

Finally, after exploring these many options, you know one thing: these questions, these constraints, all the separation, could have been spared if the U.S. government recognized your relationship with your partner.

IV. "What If": Couples Coping with the Visa System

Wendy and Belinda's Story (Part One)

Belinda Ryan and Wendy Daw © 2006 Private

Wendy Daw, a U.S. citizen, is thirty-seven; Belinda Ryan, from Britain, is forty. We listened to them on a sunny afternoon in their modest home in California's East Bay. "It's time to speak out," Belinda kept saying. They have become activists for the unrecognized rights of couples like themselves. Wendy tells how their love, and trouble, started:

> That first six months was pretty wonderful. I had just started at graduate school; Belinda had moved to this country; she was here in the Bay Area studying to be a helicopter pilot. And then she finished

> school. And that was when we started to realize the predicament: wow, this was serious.
>
> She was allowed to find a job under the student visa, so she started looking for work—but it's not that easy to find a job as a pilot. And we started to think, what will happen if she has to return to the U.K.? I had never lived with someone before. When we started living together, I felt this was a serious commitment. It crossed the line between *so I want to date* and *so I want to spend the rest of my life with her*—and what if she has to leave the country in the next week?

Belinda got her job, "just through persistence," with a jet and helicopter charter company, and a work visa with it. "And everything was OK for a while." Then, barely a year later, Belinda remembers,

> My boss said *Merry Christmas, here's your bonus, we're closing the company down.* For us, this was a catastrophe: we're going to have to look again at changing our whole life and leaving. But luckily I knew an aerial photographer. I told him: "I've got a partner here." I wasn't out to a lot of people, but I came out to him: *my partner is a woman.* He said he'd been thinking about taking someone on. … And with that I applied for a change in visa because it was a new employer.

Wendy says, "This was the fourth wrinkle in visas. About a year ago we started to add up the amount we had spent on visas. We had spent $19,000 on legal fees—the down payment on a house."

So she got this job working in aerial photography. That was all good, except—suddenly 9/11 happens. The airspace here gets shut down for three months. She can't fly. He was saying to her, "I'm just going to have to shut the business."

> To get away from it, we went to Britain for Christmas. And then—coming back—we went to go get on the airplane, this official is looking at passports, and he just suddenly pulled Belinda out of the line and told her she can't get on. And told me I *had* to get on the plane. We didn't understand, she had her visa, all her paperwork, she was totally legal.

It was a subcontractor who goes through passports. He actually called the U.S. embassy, talked to them, wouldn't let *us* talk to them. He said she couldn't get on the plane. And insisted *I* get on.

Of course we couldn't indicate we were partners. We know if it's acknowledged anywhere that she has a partner in this country, that could keep her out… Finally we left the airport. Belinda started calling. We got the automatic U.S. embassy helplines—this went on for four or five days, no human there picking up the phone, routed to a call center up in Scotland with no idea what to tell you. …

So I got on, tried every voice menu at the embassy, and after twenty-five selections I got a live person. I said*, I am an American, I need help.*

That woman helped us muddle through the whole mess. … We had to do all kinds of stuff, get something notarized—the embassy was in lockdown after 9/11, they wouldn't even let me in the door. So the notarized form and her passport had to go in by mail, and we spent days running around London, trying to get things and get them sent.

All it was, was that our lawyer had failed to tell us that even though Belinda had her work visa papers--everything legal--still, before you come back you have to send your passport and papers to the U.S. embassy in the country you're in so they can stamp it.

And no one at the airport would tell us, either, that this was the problem. For people who can't speak the language like Belinda can, or didn't have a partner: how would they find out what the problem was? We were there for an extra two weeks sorting this out. And when we get to the U.S. we can't go through the gate together: because we don't share citizenship, and can't afford to be seen as a couple.

And I went really quickly, and then had to wait and wait to see if she came through…. I'll tell you, being on the other side, and waiting and waiting for her to come through, and seeing all the others come through, and knowing that if she were turned around and sent back, there would be no way for me to find out—I had no legal right to get any information, and I knew it. None.

The incident was a crude reminder of how they lack the legal status a married couple takes for granted. Belinda says, "Even though my paperwork was good, it took me longer than two years after that before I left again. You never feel secure."

But—the skies opened up, and we carried on, but the [aerial photography] business had taken a bashing … Last year, he says to me that he can't afford to keep me on full time anymore. So I've got to make some arrangement. I thought, if he can't keep me on all the hours of my visa, I've got to leave the country. …

So I am now trying to get another job. But we are in limbo. I am in depression. Financially—if I haven't got a job by the end of next month, we have to plan our exit.[97]

Hard Choices

It is time to look at the stories of real people affected by U.S. immigration law. These include U.S. citizens such as Mark Himes, living in Pennsylvania with his French partner, who was in the last year of his six-year work visa. The couple had adopted a three-year-old boy, John, and was in the last stages of adopting a three-month-old girl, Claire Marie. Yet now, as visa expiration loomed, they confronted a possible huge threat to their home and stability. They wrote us, "We live year by year with no real plans for the future. We live in a don't-ask, don't-tell world."[98]

Mark Himes holds his daughter, Claire Marie, and son, John, while partner and co-parent Fabien takes the picture. © 2006 Private

[97] Human Rights Watch/Immigration Equality interview with Wendy Daw and Belinda Ryan, Fremont, California, January 31, 2005.

[98] E-mail to Immigration Equality from Mark Himes, August 2003.

They include people such as Luyen, twenty-four, a Taiwanese citizen, and his U.S. partner Aaron, thirty-five. Aaron had resettled in Taipei, far from his birth family and friends, so the two could remain together. Asked about U.S. immigration policy's effects on them, Luyen wrote ironically, "Nothing—besides putting us where we don't want to be and derailing our lives."[99]

Lesbian and gay binational couples are forced to make painful choices. For many, consulates and immigration offices become symbols of separation. For others, they embody bureaucratic barriers, paperwork and precariousness, time spent and legal fees paid to buy a tenuous imitation of security valid only until a visa expires: happiness on a parking meter.

Among the dilemmas couples may be forced to endure are:

- Pursuing a long-distance relationship from different countries.
- So-called "visa juggling," in which, to stay in the U.S. for as long as possible legally, the foreign-born partner switches from one non-immigrant visa to another (usually) non-immigrant visa as ability allows. For example, the foreign partner may get a tourist visa allowing a three month entry, return to her country of citizenship and re-enter the U.S. for another three months, then obtain a student visa for six months, and later try to transfer to a work visa.
- Faced with the unpalatable choice between leaving and living with the person they love in violation of U.S. immigration laws, foreign-born partners may become undocumented—staying after their visa expires.
- The U.S. partner may go into exile, leaving home for another country where they can live together legally.

All possibilities entail stress, loss, and huge expense; none promises an easy future. All these couples know, moreover, that were they heterosexual partners, U.S. immigration could quickly recognize their relationship and their right to be together. Brian and his Austrian partner Bernd, living in Colorado, struggled to find a legal way to stay together in the United States. Brian wrote us,

> Life is full of challenges, and it's too bad that this has to be one also… We live in a country full of contradictions. A country that brags about

[99] E-mail to Immigration Equality from Luyen (name changed at his request), August 2003.

being the land of the free and yet we try to oppress so many. My partner and I are law-abiding people that simply want to live our lives together, which means we need the immigration benefit provided to married couples. We're not asking for the whole world to change. We're asking for something basic; we're asking for the right to be able to love and live with the one person in the world that I want to spend the rest of my life with. That's it.[100]

[100] E-mail to Immigration Equality from Brian (last name withheld at his request), August 2003.

"My Country is Seriously Letting Me Down"

Monica, a U.S. citizen, is thirty-one, Rebecca, from the U.K., thirty. Monica is manager and trainer for a worker-owned cooperative in California. Rebecca works in computer technology back home in Britain. They were living apart when Monica wrote us:

I met Rebecca on January 31, 2003 ... We professed our love for one another on day four. I asked her to marry me on day seven and two weeks after meeting one another, we registered as domestic partners at San Francisco City Hall on February 14, 2003. What more can I say? We ran head on into our destiny. ... Since getting married we have been trying to find a way that we can simply be together and get on with our life. ...

After searching in vain for every possible way for her and I to live together permanently here in the U.S., we have found ourselves on a dead-end road. If Rebecca had lots of money to start a business here which would create jobs for Americans, if we had money for her to be able to study here or if it were even possible in the current economy to try and find an employer to sponsor her for a working visa, we would pursue one of those options. There simply isn't any way currently that we are able to live together permanently in the U.S.

Rebecca is not able to immigrate here and is only able to stay here as a tourist for up to three months at a time. I am able to go to the U.K. for up to six months at a time (as a tourist) but I cannot realistically do that yet because of my current professional and financial obligations.

She has not sought a job in the U.K.... because she met me and all we have been trying to do since then is simply be together. I have a lease, a car payment, a job that gives us a very modest income, and I have been taking care of my sister for the past year ... Rebecca has a mortgage that needs to be paid, a car loan, as well as other financial obligations in the U.K. We are trying to subsist on my income which by no means covers all of our combined financial needs, let alone try to afford plane tickets back and forth every three months and huge telephone bills!

At any time, U.S. or British customs officers could question why we are continuing to make subsequent trips to each others' countries. While they cannot keep us from entering the U.S. or U.K. because of our sexual orientations, they can keep us from entering if they suspect that there is something—or someone—that would keep us from wanting to go back to our own countries ... This last time, for example, she flew through New York City and was pulled into an interrogation room and questioned at length about her reasons for making another trip to the U.S. She was treated with blatant disrespect and was told that if she tried to return again she won't be let in ...

The thing that holds it all together is the fact that we are completely, totally, utterly, passionately, and madly in love. Most days we find ourselves feeling very strong and ready to take on the world. Some days we're not so strong and find ourselves disheartened and sad that we are not allowed the same newlywed status as other people. We should still be honeymooning, but we are so busy trying to save every penny, putting together every bit of evidence of our relationship, crossing things off our never ending to-do lists, and being activists for our cause that we always find ourselves in this constant state of exhaustion and fear ... We won't allow anyone (or any government) to separate us. We have searched way too long for one another and we now know that we simply can't live without one another.

My partner and I completely consider ourselves in every meaning of the word married. ... We have made a lifelong commitment to one another and we are now one another's reason for living. We are registered as domestic partners within the state of California, had a ceremony and have shared our happiness with our supportive partners and friends. The federal government, however, lags seriously behind on this issue of not only recognizing same-sex unions but also immigration for binational couples. We have friends (heterosexual) who met their lifelong partners in another country and were easily granted the right to marry him/her and bring them to this country to live. Men can even arrange for mail-order brides over the Internet and bring women here from other countries!

All I ask is to please open your minds and your hearts and realize that there is no difference in how gay and straight people love. The love and passion I feel for my partner is every bit as powerful and real and sacred as any straight person's. Why is that so hard to conceive of? And whatever happened to the land of the free? My country is seriously letting me down, and either it needs to evolve or it will simply be left behind.

From an e-mail from Monica (last names withheld at her request) to Immigration Equality, September 13, 2003.

Living Long Distance

Martha and Lin McDevitt-Pugh at their wedding, May 4, 2001, with the daughter of Martha's best friend's (left) and Martha's niece and nephew. (Photographer: Gon Buurman) © 2006 Private

Martha McDevitt-Pugh, who left the United States in the end to be with her life partner, Lin, told us, "You don't casually date someone across an ocean."[101] Yet many binational same-sex couples have to. Perhaps the non-U.S. partner cannot stay legally in the U.S.—or cannot even get a visa to enter it; perhaps the U.S. partner, for reasons of job or family, cannot move away. Couples hoping to build a life together are unable to create a common home. Plane tickets and phone calls become the lifelines on which a relationship survives.

Ferdinand, a Philippine citizen, met his U.S. partner Sandy over the Internet six years earlier. He was turned down by the consulate when Sandy first invited him to visit. "It

[101] Human Rights Watch/Immigration Equality telephone interview with Martha McDevitt-Pugh, founder of Love Exiles, October 10, 2005.

was a grueling experience having to undergo an application; it felt like a medieval Spanish Inquisition." In 2001, he managed to reach the United States as a tourist and they encountered face to face: "And it was magic!" They kept the relationship going on visitor's visas, flying to see each other yearly. When Ferdinand wrote us, he was applying for a student visa after acceptance into a U.S. MBA program, but was still not sure this would come through. "It is extremely difficult to sustain such an arrangement, since we both are not rich. Our resources are dwindling... We are just two people who are very much in love and would like to continue that love permanently. However, we are torn asunder by rules and inhumane laws just because we are gay men. Our only crime was that we were not born of the same country."[102]

Couples face enormous financial burdens trying to sustain a long-distance relationship—and again and again they stress how the present's pressures keep them from investing in any future. Jane, who works for the postal service in Ohio, supports her Australian partner, Laura—who cannot hold down an ordinary job at home and at the same time travel to the U.S. so that they can be together. Jane, meanwhile, cannot move to Australia because her teenage child from a previous relationship lives near her. Laura, she says,

> is only able to stay three months at a time. So every three months we go through the pain of her returning to Australia for another six weeks, or until whenever I can come up with the money for her to return. The emotional strain on us is only slightly overshadowed by the financial strain. Having to come up with $6,000 a year just for her traveling doesn't leave a lot of breathing room to pay our bills, and no room to plan for the future. ... If laws were inclusive to our situation, there would be a security that we are lacking now. She would be able to work. We could save for our future together. It would make all the difference.[103]

Harry is a teacher in Florida; Jai works as a waiter in Indonesia. Harry says, "We have been in this relationship for six years and have been able to live together only two and a half years of that time"—immediately after they met, while Jai was in the U.S. in school. "Even through the separation and loneliness we maintain our monogamous relationship... It has made our life miserable. Now money that would have been spent on making a home together is being spent on travel to be able to see him and be with him."[104]

---

[102] E-mail to Immigration Equality from Ferdinand (name changed at his request), August 2003.

[103] E-mail to Immigration Equality from Jane (name changed at her request), August 2003.

[104] E-mail to Immigration Equality from Harry (last name withheld at his request), August 2003.

"Do You Think We Don't See Through This?"

Gordon Stewart is a U.S. citizen. We interviewed him alone in New York; his partner of five years can no longer enter the United States and so remains in Brazil. He met Marcelo (not his real name) when vacationing in Rio de Janeiro in 2000—"I thought it was very auspicious that it was the first day of the new century ... So we had a long-distance relationship for several months." Then they began to discuss Marcelo coming to the United States.

He was a lawyer, well-qualified, but he didn't really speak English... I sponsored him financially, though, and he got a student visa and came in January 2001 to study English for one year. He was still doing that on September 11. I somehow figured that would change the whole scene. It did, but in delayed fashion.

In January 2002, he was accepted in St. Francis College in Brooklyn, taking law and business classes—preparing for law school in the U.S. But his student visa needed to be renewed. In May 2002, he went home to do that. I was afraid the new immigration situation might cause some problem, but he was issued a new F visa to pursue his studies.

So Marcelo completed his third semester at St. Francis, and returned to Brazil in May 2003 to renew his visa again. In June, Marcelo went to the U.S. consulate in Sao Paolo. He had all the paperwork—and suddenly the American visa officer began asking questions about his sponsor and why he was coming to the U.S. "Who is this sponsor? How did you meet him? Is he married? Are you married? Do you think we don't see through this?" His visa was rejected.

Gordon personally contacted the ambassador at the U.S. embassy to Brazil:

The officer who rejected him writes me in a proud email: "This guy in his mid-twenties"—Marcelo was thirty-nine—"says he wants to study in the U.S. at some unknown university." He said this was not a bona fide student visa application: he has other reasons to be there. And he said, "What you need is a good immigration lawyer: good luck." It was evident that they absolutely did not read the application: "This guy says he wants to go study in the U.S.": he already had been there studying! You just want to scream at these people.

I responded, "I respectfully disagree," gave the chronology, said it was an appropriate course of study for what he was trying to do. He wrote back—tell the applicant to reapply; he will have another visa officer, good luck

They were rejecting him because he had "immigrant intent," though they hadn't said it yet. Marcelo had worked for the now governor of Sao Paolo state, who wrote a letter saying he had ties there still. Marcelo and the ambassador thought that was pretty good. I was skeptical.

Marcelo goes in for a new interview. The officer, a woman, calls a man over to look at the application. He says, "This is not legitimate. Cancel the visa." It's obvious in retrospect that they rejected him on the basis of his appearance and the "oddity" of being sponsored by an "older single man."

Through a lawyer, we found out that the guy who rejected him first was the head visa officer; obviously the reapplication was a fraud, setup, façade—on which he had to spend $300 in application fees.

We engaged a lawyer, wrote the consul general—he rejected it immediately: they said, we are not looking at this case further. The ambassador herself wrote to me and said, these people report to Homeland Security, not to me: there is nothing I can do.

For the first month, I couldn't sleep at all. We had bought an apartment here. We were thinking, this was our life—we would be together. All his stuff is in it. He went home for three weeks and he has never been able to come back. It's crazy. I haven't spent more than one weekend in the apartment since. I can't stand being there. It's just the fact of not being together, of having dreamed of being together.

Since then, I call Marcelo every day, and it's a hassle and you have to find the calling cards and Marcelo spends a fair amount of money on calling cards too. If I didn't have resources, the relationship never would have worked out—it would be too expensive, difficult and costly, emotionally and financially.

And since then I have gone to Brazil every other weekend, basically. We're extremely lucky that I have the resources to go back and forth. That puts me in the top one-percent category as far as suffering is concerned—and even at that it's not been easy. There's personal strain: we can spend the weekend together but that means I have a ten-hour flight on Friday night and a ten-hour flight on Sunday night and the flight arrives at 6 a.m. Monday morning and I have to be at work by 8. And we're on different schedules, wavelengths, I'm always jet-lagged when we meet, and it's so difficult to connect. I get to Brazil on a Saturday morning and he may have things he wants to do and sometimes all I want to do is sleep. And there's the strain of trying to maintain my friends and family contacts in the U.S. because I am always going to Brazil. I cannot lead a normal personal life because I am spending so much time in airplanes to sustain my relationship. He is waiting for something to happen that will solve the problem and there is nothing he can do. We both suffer the strain.

My company has agreed to transfer me to the U.K. and he will go there. But, he still has nightmares about the rejection—they did it in such a public way, forty people in the room and the consul yelling at him, "Do you think we don't see through this?" He was totally humiliated.

The inequality is obvious. I felt I had always been privileged for my entire life, and always tried to understand other people's circumstances from without—and when this happened it just clearly showed me what prejudice, bias, injustice is: because it's totally, completely unfair.

And I feel ashamed that he comes from a country that is supposedly a "developing," often belittled country, and yet they have gone forward and supported gay people and human rights in so many different ways. It's embarrassing. I haven't focused a lot on being angry, because I have to keep my energy focused on keeping the relationship together—on travel, on literally staying awake. The last thing I want to do is to get on a crammed plane, economy class, for ten hours to go to Brazil tomorrow. But I'm glad I can do it. I would go every weekend if I could. If this isn't a commitment to a relationship I don't know what is a commitment to a relationship. And the fact that they don't recognize or respect that kind of commitment, is just beyond me.

From a Human Rights Watch/Immigration Equality interview with Gordon Stewart, New York, November 23, 2004.

Juggling Visas

Struggling to stay together legally in the U.S., many foreign partners in same-sex relationships juggle visa options—tourist, student, or work. Their lives become an alphabet soup, with maintaining or moving to B, F, or H status an almost daily, draining obsession.

Lynnette, a special education teacher in California, tells a typical story. She fell in love with Mei-ling, from Taiwan, a printmaker and painter, who now works as an art instructor for the disabled. It is particularly difficult to adjust non-immigrant visas to immigrant status:

> She has had a practical training visa, then an H1B visa (both non-immigrant visas) and is now filing for a change in status to get a green card. It took four lawyers and constant negotiation with her employer to get to this point. It has made our stay together stressful, unsettling (how can you settle down if you don't know where you can live or stay?) and expensive. It has been demoralizing to see how little our relationship means legally. We mean so much to each other but nothing to my government, even though we are contributing members of society.[105]

People using student or training visas to stay with their partner often find themselves forcibly infantilized—regressing to seek a redundant education. The costs of staying in school can be acute, since most student visas allow limited opportunity to work; the U.S. partner must frequently furnish tuition and support. Moreover, foreign students usually cannot get financial aid, and even at state institutions pay several times what in-state residents do—an inequity remediable if their relationships were acknowledged to permit them residency.

Gillian and her partner Sariya, from Thailand, met while the latter was studying in the U.S.: "We fell in love and have been together ever since. That was almost five years ago." Living on a student visa has been difficult, though, "adding stress and uncertainty; making it necessary for Sariya to stay in school without a break at a cost to her stress level and our finances."[106] Rebecca, twenty-seven, wrote us about her three-year

---

[105] E-mail to Immigration Equality from Lynnette (name changed at her request), August 19, 2003.

[106] E-mail to Immigration Equality from Gillian and Sariya (last names withheld at their request), August 23, 2003.

relationship with her U.K. partner, Eileen. Each summer, Eileen comes to the U.S. on a training visa to serve in a summer camp, and Rebecca works there to be with her.

> We have both essentially put our professional lives on hold to be together. … It is difficult to explain to loved ones that I am going back to work at camp for one more year—when they (and I) know that I could get a full-time year-round job elsewhere that would allow me to start saving for retirement and a house. As it is now, we basically scrape to get by.[107]

To make ends meet, some are forced to violate the terms of their visas by working. The job is almost always poorly paid. Tony, a social worker from Brooklyn, met his Brazilian partner while Miguel was visiting New York. "We were forced to maintain a long-distance relationship for three years until Miguel could get a student visa," Tony says:

> He was a public defender in Brazil; when he got here with his visa, which precludes work, he was only able to take the occasional house-cleaning job. Oh, wait, did I say he was a lawyer in Brazil and had to work as a house cleaner in New York City? … His choosing to come here on a student visa has plummeted him into a regressed role as student. Had he been my spouse he could have looked for work. If Hillary Clinton had to clean toilet bowls that might jolt her esteem too. As for me, it has been stressful at times bearing a large financial burden… We constantly have to sit with "what if."[108]

---

[107] E-mail to Immigration Equality from Rebecca (last names withheld at her request), September 13, 2003.

[108] E-mail to Immigration Equality from Tony (name changed at his request), September 2, 2003.

"I Can Buy a House Here ... But I Just Can't Live My Life in It"

Will and Stefano have been committed partners for a decade and a half. Will is a US citizen; Stefano has dual Australian-Italian nationality, born of Italian parents who had recently migrated down under when he was born. The couple fell in love while Will was working in Sydney on a business visa. "We met at a dance party with fifteen thousand people there, gay and lesbian Mardi Gras. We danced till 6 a.m., exchanged phone numbers using the eyeliner of a drag queen at the coat check, and have been together ever since."

They live in the United States now, where Will works for a large corporation, and have adopted a child. But, they have had a perpetual struggle to keep Stefano in status so that Will can keep his job here, and they can stay together.

For five years Stefano has been taking college courses, working to complete a B.A. in fashion and merchandising. Will says: "What is most annoying is instead of his being able to work and contribute his talents to this country, he has to spend his time in school and we are actually having to pay for him to be here." Stefano elaborates:

In order to be with Will, I haven't been able to work since 1996. And I pay more at the state university as an international student. We owned a home in state, and I was a state resident, but at school I was an international student. Any state resident who was a U.S. citizen would pay $1,500 a semester; we were paying close to $10,000 a semester for me to attend school.

It's so strange. I can buy a house here—they are fine when I pay taxes. But I just can't live my life in it.

Stefano is faced with his student visa expiring and decisions loom. Will formally adopted their son Evan, from China, fourteen months old when we talked to them, in 2003:

We found an adoption agency that we knew was not openly discriminatory towards gays and lesbians. They cared only about improving the life of an orphaned child. I submitted my application as a single, unmarried male. Now we are going through the process of second-parent adoption for Stefano. Our lawyer already told us this will affect Stefano's status: by adopting an American citizen, he will be making clear his intention to stay. So our son, who seals our commitment to each other, might seal our separation. Stefano may never get a visa again.

But they have already burnt their bridges—by crossing one: publicly declaring their relationship by celebrating their marriage, across a river in Canada, in 2003. "We were married in Niagara Falls, Ontario. Our wedding invitations and wedding bands say, 'Head over falls in love.'" Now they have begun the process of emigrating to Canada. Will says, "Having a child made us realize that we need to find a home that will be home, a place where we can be for fifteen years and be secure."

Stefano corrects him: "I knew even before we had a child that I definitely wanted to leave. I don't like it here any more." Will adds,

I no longer feel committed to this country. We want to be in a country whose values align more closely with the values of our family, so that as we raise our son, he doesn't question why his parents are out of status, unusual, discriminated against.

"It's only recently I broached with my mother the concept of being Canadian," Will says.

I think this whole experience has opened up her eyes. She's always been a very proud American, proud of what this country stood for; my brother fought in the first Gulf War; and every time we talk with her she tries to defend America, it's not so bad, *and I think it's only recently she's beginning to say,* this sucks. Three very important people in my life are most likely now going to be leaving this country because of this. *All of our friends and family echo that. Shameful that this is supposed to be one of the most progressive countries, founded on the concept of democracy, and here is this one essential fact: we are in love and we can't live here.*

While we interviewed the couple, Evan played quietly in the background, and three dogs roamed the room—beautiful Australian beagles which, Will explained, were thirteen years old: "We've had them since our first year together in Sydney, and they have followed us ever since."

When we came together to the U.S. to live, we brought them with us; they got a vet test that entitled them to travel with us, and were put in a crate on the same flight. When we landed in the U.S., we waited by the baggage carousel and they brought up our crates, and then a wildlife inspector trundled by—a middle-aged woman, sort of small and crotchety. She bent over, looked into the cage, and said, "Aren't they cute!" And that's all it took: that's how they got into the country. So it is easier to get my dog permanent residency than my partner of fourteen years.

From a Human Rights Watch/Immigration Equality interview with Will and Stefano (names changed at their request), New York City, January 19, 2005.

Those in the U.S. on work visas face different, equally difficult challenges. There is the constant fear that if the visa-holder loses the job, he or she will be forced to return home—meaning separation or dislocation for the couple.

As discussed above, finding an employer willing to sponsor a foreigner can be hard. The hirer must expend vastly more effort than taking on an U.S. citizen entails. The authorities have near-absolute leeway to reject work visa applications; requests can languish in endless delay. From Connecticut, Rich related how his Polish partner Greg, studying business, tried to get a work visa for a job in his family's U.S. firm. The then INS turned him down, Rich reports,

> saying the business was too small to need a college-educated person in the management role they were offering. Since his family owns several other businesses, we appealed, explaining the business was larger than the application would lead one to believe… In February of 2003 Greg's case suddenly got transferred to the INS in Washington. … Greg spoke with the INS weeks ago and they informed him it can take a year from the date the case moved to Washington for his appeal to be answered. So, we are left in limbo. If his work visa is not approved, we would be separated and I would be powerless to help. I don't even want to think

about it! My family would be devastated if I had to move out of the U.S. This entire situation is just horrid.[109]

Both partners' careers may suffer in trying to stay together. When Maggie wrote us, she had left her North Carolina home to live in Australia with her lover Sarah. Both were computer programmers who met while Sarah was in the United States, and had struggled to remain there: "We researched our options, but the most promising ways to allow her to stay would have required her to take up careers she had absolutely no interest in (nursing, for instance) or attempt to go to college in the U.S. and somehow pay for that. That's no way to live your life, spending your days playing at something you have no interest in just to be with the one you love."[110]

Stopped at the Gate: Harassment by Immigration Authorities

Whether traveling to meet, or trying to keep the foreign partner legally in the U.S., couples fear the power of U.S. immigration officers to break up their lives by stopping them at the border. Crossing customs is a constant reminder of how fragile their relationships are, absent legal recognition.

Stephanie and Callie on a visit to Callie's hometown in Oregon. © 2006 Private

Stephanie and Callie have been partners since 2003. Stephanie is a U.K. citizen, Callie from the U.S. For the first year, they exchanged visits, managing to spend months together at a time—but always knowing the days were limited. Stephanie says, "The airport is just the worst thing .... You always worry that you're looking too shifty when

---

[109] E-mail to Immigration Equality from Rich (last name withheld at his request), November 13, 2003.

[110] E-mail to Immigration Equality from Maggie (last name withheld at her request), September 4, 2003.

you're going through. You constantly worry you'll be turned away, although you're doing nothing."[111] Callie adds:

> We were always careful if we were traveling together not to carry any documents that showed us as a couple together, in any way. No letters, cards, photos even… We didn't want to get caught—no, not "caught," because we weren't doing anything illegal. We never considered breaking the law, because we both wanted to do it completely legally.[112]

Other couples, however intent on legality, have worse stories to tell. Thomas, twenty-eight, lives in Chicago, an ocean and half a continent away from his French partner of eight years, Francois. They met while Thomas was studying in Paris as a college junior, were able to live together in France when Thomas returned there for graduate school, but then had to separate when he got a teaching job at home. "That was two and a half years ago, and we still have not found a way to bring Francois to the U.S. to live." They visit and vacation together; Thomas remembers how, returning to the U.S. from a joint trip to Canada,

> I had to go through separately because we're not considered a family, and I stood on the other side while one official was giving Francois a really hard time, asking probing questions that were not even relevant. Francois was not at liberty to say that my boyfriend did a really nice thing and bought me a present [this surprise trip to Canada] – he was worried that this would incur even worse treatment. The immigration official demanded proof that he would return to France, but Francois didn't have his plane ticket on him, so the official wasn't even going to allow him back into the U.S. Technically—we weren't aware of this—he has to carry it with him always to prove his intent to leave. I was standing at a distance watching, feeling powerless. The immigration official saw me and said that I couldn't even stand there—and berated him. I had to move away till I wasn't visible; it revealed that we were a couple. He treated him differently—smirking, laughing, treating him with disgust. After all this, he just said, *Take your papers and leave,* and he let him through. It was all about his own power.

---

[111] Human Rights Watch/Immigration Equality telephone interview with Stephanie and Callie (names changed at their request), October 12, 2005.

[112] Ibid.

> Then I think, *this man represents my country*— is this a country that I want to be associated with? Do I want to bring Francois to the U.S. if this is how he is going to be treated? This is where I want to live because it's where my family is, but does this place represent the values that we have?[113]

Gitte Bossi-Andresen, a Danish citizen, was detained twice while entering the U.S. to visit her American partner of almost eighteen years, Kelly. "They asked me why I was going to school, what I was doing there, if I could prove it, why I had left the states, why I was coming back… I was bombarded with questions." Near tears, she says:

> As a kid, I was always told, you are a diplomat for your country, you're a diplomat for your family, so when you go out, you behave in that way. So being detained, treated and singled as a criminal, it really means something to me. Maybe those incidents don't have to do with directly with me being gay, but they do indirectly: had I not been gay, I would have been married.[114]

The passport record of visits that keep a relationship going can turn incriminating at immigration control. Nathalie Fuz remembers how once JFK immigration "held me for an hour, asking why I was going back and forth so much, grilling me about the multiple entries. … I always get nervous when I enter the country. They are not pleasant." Her U.S. partner, Kelly, says, "It's always nerve-wracking." When they cross the northern border for a trip, "There's this Peace Bridge between Canada and the U.S., and now ironically we feel this whole anxiety about crossing the Peace Bridge to come back. We can't eliminate the factor that our relationship isn't valid. You feel totally suspect."[115]

---

[113] Human Rights Watch telephone interview with Thomas (names changed at his request), October 26, 2005.

[114] Human Rights Watch/Immigration Equality telephone interview with Gitte Bossi-Andresen and Kelly Bossi-Andresen, December 20, 2005.

[115] Human Rights Watch/Immigration Equality interview with Nathalie Fuz and Kelly McGowan, New York, October 14, 2005.

Deported

Many couples fear immigration officers, but Asa and Tony have a particularly horrible story. Asa, a British citizen, was deported while trying to visit Tony in the U.S., and Homeland Security launched its own investigation of their relationship.

Tony, forty and a denizen of Atlanta, Georgia, met Asa, thirty-three, during a vacation in Britain in early 2002. They fell in love, and, like many other couples, immediately faced a quandary: how to be together?

At the time, U.K. immigration laws gave residency to unmarried foreign partners of British citizens—but only after the couple had lived together for two years. The two therefore planned eventually to move to London, but since Tony had commitments to his own business in the U.S., they would need to demonstrate their cohabitation through Asa spending as much time as possible with him there. "I went to the INS," Asa says, "and they told me there was no limit to how often I could come in and out of the U.S. legally, as long as I don't overstay. So I would go in and out of the county every ninety days."

I spent the majority of my time during those two years in the U.S... While I was forced to quit my job in Britain to spend time in the States, I could not work, drive, own a cell phone or even a bank account in America—all the things most people take for granted. My partner was powerless to do anything to help. ... One of our major hurdles was that I had to live in America [to prove to the U.K. that they had cohabited for two years], but I couldn't do so legally in the U.S.'s eyes. Yet, we had to build documentation that we were living together. We had to walk this fine line.

Still, Asa left every three months and remained legal. In 2004, having met the requirements, they resettled in London, where Tony got a new job. In June 2005, Tony had to return to the U.S. for an eight-week business trip—"which was a long time to be apart," Asa says. "We said I'd go there on holiday for two weeks [at the end of Tony's trip], and fly back together. Tony asked me if I was worried about coming into the country. Ironically, every other time I was horrified coming into the country, the most nerve-wracking experience. This time, I wasn't worried at all."

At the Atlanta airport, "I got to immigration. They asked me the standard series of questions: last time I was here, what I was here for—a holiday. I kept the answers as simple as possible. They put my passport in an orange folder, so I knew. They took me into another room."

That was the horrible experience in itself… There was an African woman who had a little baby and they were letting the baby into the country and not the mother. And then they had a few other people who'd been put aside for questioning as well. At least I spoke English—I could tell the translators weren't doing a proper job interpreting.

They asked details about me. I told them the hundred percent truth. I said I'm in a same-sex relationship, we live in the U.K., we transferred our lives there … It was blatantly obvious to me that the questioning was homophobic. It's hard to explain… You knew they could do it because our relationship had no status, and the end result was that it all happened to me because I was in a same-sex relationship … I guess I just wasn't human.

He asked me questions about our landlord when we had lived in San Francisco. Were they already investigating us? He told me that he didn't think I'd be let into the country. I said, "Don't do this to me."

They never said, You have been refused entry because. *And I never actually asked, why aren't you letting me in. I just said, please, don't do this to me. I was given a refusal, and made to sign. The flights to the U.K. were all booked. They didn't think they could permit me to fly back to another E.U. country. They found a London flight leaving in a couple of hours, with one seat in first class—for $5,000. I bought that. When my flight came up, I got escorted there by a Homeland Security officer and boarded onto the plane.*

"The American government has singled gay people out for mistreatment," Asa says. "We have been careful to abide by every law and hurdle placed in front of us, and we are still being treated as criminals."

Tony waited hours for Asa to emerge—then waited for him to call when he got back to London that night. He remembers,

At 10 or 11 a.m. next morning, someone was banging on my door—two officers standing there, cars sitting in front of my house. I was shocked. But I knew what it was. Homeland Security.

[The agents] didn't want any pleasant communications. They informed me of my rights—I could have an attorney present; they recorded everything. I told them all they asked for. They wanted to know what my relationship to Asa was. I knew he'd already told them, so I told them the same.

They knew things about our relationship. We had moved to San Francisco for about a year. We'd signed a lease there, so we had both our names on it. Sitting in my house, they had the documentation: they asked about our landlords in San Francisco by name; "Did Asa live with you for the year?" I explained that no, he'd been doing it legally, leaving and entering every ninety days. They didn't believe me. They asked, "Where are you living now?" I said in London. Obviously, they didn't believe I was living anywhere but Atlanta, because I still own the house there. The line of questioning was: when did we meet; how long in was he in the U.S.; did I know that it was a violation of law if I let him live with me and if I harbored an illegal immigrant? They asked me how Asa supported himself in the U.S. They knew he didn't have a job in the U.K. "So he lives there but you pay all the bills?"

By coincidence or not, Tony says, "One or two weeks later, I got an internal revenue audit. That's still going on… I'm not at risk, but—I suspect that they're making sure that I didn't pay Asa."

"We never did anything that should have flagged us," Tony says. "Honestly, I love my country; if we could live in America tomorrow, I would want to come home. …Our home is there. My family is there. Asa's family is spread out. He and I are here alone in London." And yet, Tony says, "they treat me so well over here, almost to the point that it freaks you out. It's the other side of the spectrum. You don't see any hate here. It's really nice."

From a Human Rights Watch/Immigration Equality telephone interview with Asa and Tony (last names withheld at their request), January 5, 2006, and an e-mail from Asa to Human Rights Watch, January 5, 2006.

Seeking Safety and "Looking Gay": The Asylum System

Some foreign partners know that, because of their sexuality, at home they would face violence, arrest, or death. Yet in claiming asylum, they do not always find a full or sympathetic hearing.

In one well-known case, Jorge Soto Vega, from Tuxpan, Mexico, had suffered violence in his community and even family since childhood. Police severely beat him, threatening to kill him unless he left—because, they said, they wanted to cleanse the town of gay people.

In 2002 in the U.S., Soto Vega claimed asylum. Immigration judge John Taylor found credible evidence that he was persecuted in Mexico because of his sexual orientation—yet threw out his claim. Soto Vega, he said, looked straight and could hide his sexual orientation if he chose. Taylor wrote: "It seems to me that if he returned to Mexico in some other community, that it would not be obvious that he would be homosexual unless he made that ... obvious himself."[116]

Both the confidence in stereotypes, and the belief that the closet can guarantee both sanity and safety, remain rife in the immigration system. Tom Smeraldo lives in New Jersey with his Venezuelan partner of four years, Emilio Ojeda. In 2002, Emilio first learned that it was possible to claim asylum from sexual-orientation-based persecution. At his hearing in late 2003, Tom says, "The officer asked offensive questions—clearly she was not trained; for instance, 'when did you start *acting* gay?'" Emilio says,

> Anyone investigating asylum for sexual orientation should know better than to ask the questions she did. The implication was, you are faking that you are gay. … Immigration is looking for the stereotypes; for instance, a judge said to a friend of mine who was making a claim, "You don't look like a lesbian." They assume that all immigrants are straight and all asylum-seekers on the basis of sexual orientation are frauds or criminals.

---

[116] *Soto Vega v. Ashcroft*, No. 04-70868. The case remains on appeal.

Tom Smeraldo and Emilio Ojeda in 2006 in their home. © 2006 Private

Emilio appealed a deportation order. On October 11, 2005, the case was postponed for six more months. Before that, Tom told us that "I don't know how long we can live like this. If Emilio loses, we'll apply immediately for Canadian immigration. I would love to be treated equally somewhere, and I don't want to die living my life as a second class citizen."[117]

Giovanni was beginning to work for LGBT rights in his provincial city in Colombia when he met his partner Mark, a U.S. citizen, in 2001. Mark encouraged him to be more vocal. Giovanni says he and a few colleagues sent a letter to the guerilla group FARC, urging them to stop violence against homosexuals. Death threats followed; after a public meeting, a group of men attacked, clubbed, and whipped him, leaving him unconscious and with permanent injuries.

Mark helped him get a training visa to the U.S., and Giovanni relocated in 2003. They began preparing an asylum claim—a costly, time-consuming process. Giovanni was

[117] Human Rights Watch/Immigration Equality telephone interview with Emilio Ojeda and Tom Smeraldo, October 6, 2005.

admitted to Bellevue Hospital's program for torture survivors; doctors documented his injuries from the beating. Yet at his interview, he stared at a "stern face":

> I knew that it was going to turn out badly. When I said the word "homosexual" his face grew hard. He never looked at me. I had read about Soto Vega and so I tried to look more "gay." I'd shaved my mustache and tried to fit the stereotypes. … At the end I said, "I'm talking, sir, with my heart, I'm telling you the truth." I said, "Please help me, I'm gay, my life is hell in that country."[118]

The written Notice of Intent to Deny refusing his claim, which Giovanni received weeks later, contained troubling phrases: "the teacher told you that he knew you were a faggot"; "you were warned that [you] would be killed because [you] were a faggot."[119] Both Giovanni and Mark were disturbed to find the word "faggot" used without quotation marks in an official U.S. government document.

Giovanni appealed. Eventually, a perhaps-embarrassed INS overturned the decision. However, he reflects resentfully on how abject the experience left him.

> I got tortured, went to an embassy three times, I got a visa, I came to this country with my horrible English. I arrived and lived with my boyfriend. I applied for asylum, I waited for a long time with no response, I was denied and then approved. One woman from Colombia finds a man and marries him and in one year she is an American resident. Do you think that is fair?

Mark agrees: "I'm not asking for special rights. I'm just asking to be equal."[120]

Lives Not in Order: The Undocumented

Undocumented immigrants are the main focus of current attempts to reform—or radically restrict—immigration. But what does it actually mean to be undocumented? It

---

[118] Human Rights Watch/Immigration Equality interview with Giovanni and Mark (last names withheld at their request), New York, August 18, 2004.

[119] "Notice of Intent to Deny," Newark Asylum Office, date and name withheld at the applicant's request, copy on file with Human Rights Watch and Immigration Equality.

[120] Human Rights Watch/Immigration Equality interview with Giovanni and Mark (last names withheld at their request), August 18, 2004.

describes a foreign national who is not in the U.S. on a valid visa. There are several ways of becoming undocumented.

First, a person may cross a U.S. border without an entry visa. "Entrance without inspection" happens mainly along the Canadian and Mexican borders. It has become the popular image of "illegal" immigrants, but this actually is much less common than other ways of becoming undocumented. More usually, one enters on a valid visa such as a student or work visa, and overstays its term. A student, for instance, would begin to "accrue unlawful presence" when she no longer attends a university but remains in the United States. [121]

An undocumented immigrant who accumulates from 180 days to a year of unlawful presence is barred for three years from returning to the United States. An undocumented immigrant who accrues unlawful presence of more than a year is subject to a ten-year bar. Ways exist to overcome the bars to returning, including (in some cases) marrying a U.S. citizen, but—again—this is not available to lesbian and gay families.

Lesbians and gays arguably have fewer possibilities than most other immigrants to obtain legal presence here. Moreover, it may also be difficult for the U.S. partner to move abroad. More formidable obstacles than work and family ties may intervene. Foreign laws may not acknowledge their partnership. The U.S. partner may not have the education or background to be accepted permanently in a country where immigration law and policy favor skills over family ties.

Thus, many find themselves boxed into the difficult decision to stay together in the U.S. where the foreign partner is "unlawful." No one wants this. Undocumented foreign partners told us they had actively tried to keep in regular status but could find no alternatives that would preserve the relationship. Fearing they might be forced into it, Stephanie and Callie told us that "Overstaying your visa is not like killing someone; it's just staying to be with the one you love. Yet you're treated as a criminal."[122] For most, going undocumented means a life of privation, immobility, and fear.

---

[121] The Immigration and Nationality Act defines unlawful presence as follows: "An alien is deemed to be unlawfully present in the United States if the alien is present in the United States after the expiration of the period of stay authorized by the Attorney General (Secretary of Homeland Security) or is present in the United States without being admitted or paroled."

[122] Human Rights Watch/Immigration Equality telephone interview with Stephanie and Callie (names changed at their request), October 12, 2005.

"A Constant, Gnawing Fear"

Tara, a U.S. citizen, twenty-four, and Stacy, her Canadian partner, twenty-five, lived in small-town Appalachia when they wrote us, and had been together for three years. Stacy is undocumented. They stayed together in the U.S. because Tara, studying and working in market research, was in a far better position to support them than Stacy would be in Canada. Tara says, "There are no steps available for us to live together here legally. She does not have a college degree, Canada is not in the green card lottery, and she has no relations in the U.S. You would think our northern neighbors would have an easy time getting into the U.S. for good, but that is not the case."

I can't begin to describe it. We suffer financially because she must work at a horrible job that has already once ruined her health. Because of the "dirt" her employers have on her legal status here, she has to take whatever hours they give her, which vary from too many humanly possible to barely double digits a week. She could easily have a job where I work that would pay much better and be easier on her body, but can't due to her legal status here. Not having to stay on her feet all day and carry heavy loads would do wonders for her health.

It's almost impossible for us to visit her family ... Every time we cross the border, we know we risk her not being allowed back in the country. Her aunt died almost a year ago. She did not get to see her one last time for fear that the post-9/11 border would not let her return. She took this pretty hard, as did I.

There is a constant, gnawing fear any time we see any official of the law. Whenever someone knocks on the door unexpectedly, we both jump, panicked, wondering if it's INS or other government officials, finally catching up with us... It's very hard knowing someone can rip you away from the one you love at any time.

We don't participate in many public activities together for fear of being turned in. ... Almost a year ago, Stacy sustained a serious back injury. We went to hospitals in the US, but considering she has no health insurance here, not much was done. The condition worsened to a point that we made an emergency trip to her hometown in Canada to see a doctor that would actually look at her injury and take it seriously. As a result, she had surgery, almost a month of inpatient therapy, and still has a permanent limp because of this condition, which could have been averted had she been given proper medical care from the outset.

We dropped to barely one income since I was going to school full time and working hardly any hours at my job, and because of her uncertain legal status she was in no way eligible for any aid whatsoever. Imagine being taken off work for six months with no income, not even workers' comp or unemployment.

I am still trying to pay off debt from this period of our lives. This isn't a story begging for your pity, merely an example of how a binational couple must live. We have no rights, we know we can be forced into separation at any moment (I imagine there are stiff penalties for one such as myself who helps an illegal live in the U.S. for so long), all because we had the good fortune to be two women who love each other more than anything.

If we are ever caught and forced to separate, I don't know what I'd do. She is my life, my love, everything I've ever wanted in a woman... She gave up everything, and I do mean everything, to live here with me. When she came over the border she had a backpack of clothing and nothing else. Everything we have together now we built up together. It's not her clothing and my clothing, separated, it's our clothing, our computer, our television, our dog. ... Oddly enough, we hardly ever fight, especially about money or our situation. We just love each other, and couldn't imagine not being together.

We're normal, nice people who don't do much out of the ordinary. It strikes both us and our friends as humorous, in a twisted way, that we've broken so many federal laws over something as silly as us being allowed to live together.

From an e-mail to Immigration Equality from Tara and Stacy (names changed at their request), October 20, 2003

The undocumented are trapped here, usually unable to leave the U.S. without facing legal bars to their return. Stephen told us of his European partner, who had been in the country since 1995: "It has put a lot of stress on our relationship with fears that immigration will show up and deport him. There is also the stress that he has not seen his family in seven years, whom he is extremely close with. He (we) missed the marriage of his sister and the birth of two nephews from two of his brothers. There is also the fact that his parents are elderly and if one died he would not be able to leave the country for the funeral, for fear of not being allowed back in. We are a committed couple in every sense of the word. We recently celebrated eight years together."[123]

[123] E-mail to Immigration Equality from Stephen (names changed at his request), undated, 2003.

Chet, sixty-seven, and his Taiwanese partner Wei, fifty-nine, had been committed partners for two decades, during most of which Wei had lived in the U.S. undocumented: "We have lived together and been devoted to each other for the last twenty years and have tried every way possible to get him permanent residence… Every possibility has been a dead end because of immigration laws against gay partners." In that time, Wei had been able to visit Taiwan only twice to see his ailing mother; confusion about the order of his names in his passport meant that his overstay was not in the records, and allowed him to return. "His mother passed away two years ago but he could not chance returning for the funeral for fear he would not get another visa." Now Chet fears that if he dies, Wei could be deported if he comes forward as an heir. "We live day to day praying that the immigration laws will change and we can live together in peace without the constant fear that something will happen that will cause his deportation."[124]

Detention, and deportation after it, indeed menace the undocumented. Immigration detention has ballooned in the U.S. since September 11. (Whereas in 1995, 33,000 people were deported and some 5,500 were held by immigration authorities on an average day, in 2003, more than 77,000 were deported and 20,000 detained on an average day.[125]) Human Rights Watch has repeatedly drawn attention to unacceptable conditions in detention centers—many of which are local jails, or contracted centers run by private corrections companies. [126] Standards for immigration detention centers exist, but are inadequately and irregularly implemented.[127] Immigration Equality's work with lesbian, gay, bisexual, and transgender immigrants has shown patterns of harassment, discrimination, and abuse in detention. HIV-positive detainees also face discriminatory treatment, including denial of medications and placement in twenty-three-hour lockdown if they self-identify—clearly discouraging them from coming forward and seeking treatment.

---

[124] E-mail to Immigration Equality from Chet (names changed at his request), September 1, 2003.

[125] Bryan Lonegan et.al, "Immigration Detention and Removal: A Guide for Detainees and Their Families," Immigration Law Unit of the Legal Aid Society, October 2004, p. 1. A documented immigrant who commits two or more "crimes of moral turpitude" while in the U.S. can also be detained and subjected to removal proceedings. This can include arrest and conviction for "indecency" or "soliciting" by police entrapment in cruising areas, among other "morals" offenses.

[126] See, for instance, "Letter to INS Commissioner Doris Meissner," Human Rights Watch, October 30, 2004, at http://hrw.org/english/docs/2000/10/30/usdom649.htm, "Detained and Deprived of Rights: Children in the Custody of the U.S. Immigration and Naturalization Service," A Human Rights Watch Report, vol. 10, no. 4 (G), December 1998, and "Locked Away: Immigration Detainees in Jails in the United States," A Human Rights Watch Report, vol. 10, no. 1 (G), September 1998.

[127] See U.S. Immigration and Customs Enforcement's "Detention Operations Manual," online at http://www.ice.gov/graphics/dro/opsmanual/index.htm (retrieved January 9, 2006).

The non-recognition of lesbian, gay, bisexual, or transgender people's relationships can also weigh against foreign partners facing removal proceedings. Eligibility for bond (that is, release from immigration detention) for people who have received a removal order, and applications for cancellation of removal, can, in some cases, be influenced by whether the person has a family member—spouse, parent, or child—who is a U.S. citizen or permanent resident. This is particularly so if the deportation would cause the family member "exceptional and extremely unusual hardship." DOMA codified that same-sex partners cannot qualify as family members for these purposes.[128]

To stem the fears that come with being undocumented, some couples contemplate a sham opposite-sex marriage for the foreign partner. The idea of entering into a fraudulent partnership only because the government will not recognize their real one infuriates and humiliates many. Amy, living with her British partner in San Francisco, feared they would have to separate when a student visa expired:

> Now I think if we want to stay in California, an arranged marriage is the only option we can afford. If we're found out, the non-U.S. citizen is kicked out of the U.S. forever and the U.S. husband can be put in jail or fined. But, as a gay person, I don't want to live a lie. The idea of having to be at my girlfriend's wedding is just a day I don't know how I would get through.[129]

Wade Nichols and Francis Shen in 2002 on their honeymoon. © 2006 Private

[128] Many heterosexual families face separation under these provisions as well, both because certain grounds for removal prohibit considering family ties, and because the standard for "exceptional and extremely unusual hardship" has been set increasingly high by recent Board of Immigration Appeals decisions.

[129] Human Rights Watch/Immigration Equality telephone interview with Amy (name changed at her request), October 25, 2005.

Wade Nichols and his Taiwanese partner Francis Shen, living together in what for Wade is exile in Taipei, had considered a fake marriage to stay together in the U.S. Francis has been harassed by U.S. immigration before. He says marrying is "a long shot, and then I'd have to go through immigration again, but that time it would be more difficult because I'd be lying. It was hard enough when I wasn't lying. … It's insane," he adds. "The government would rather have people lie to them than be honest with them."[130]

"And Then It Was All Taken From Me"

Ricardo Espíndola and Wayne Brown © 2006 Private

Wayne Brown, forty-seven, a clinical social worker, lives in Florida at the moment. His partner Ricardo Espíndola is from Argentina and is unemployed. Wayne, a Canadian citizen, had been a lawful permanent U.S. resident for many years, working as program director of a large HIV/AIDS service group.

[130] Human Rights Watch/Immigration Equality telephone interview with Wayne Nichols and Francis Shen, November 2, 2005.

Ricardo came to the United States in 2000 on a three-month visa waiver available to Argentineans. He found work; he stayed; he met Wayne. The two had launched the paperwork to have their partnership recognized for immigration purposes in Canada, and planned eventually to move there and be fully legal. Things took a wrong turn in late 2004 on a desert highway. Ricardo's undocumented status came back to haunt him—and the couple was ripped apart.

"We traveled through the U.S. in the course of our years living together," Wayne said. "This was just one other trip that we had planned. On September 21, we flew into Albuquerque, and we left early the next day to drive to southern New Mexico."

We were out in the desert. We saw a barrier—we thought it was the park entrance we were headed to. Ricardo was driving. He rolled up to the gate. Then we realized they were border patrol. We just froze. We were in shock. We didn't expect a random stop. If I had known that border patrol could stop anyone within 100 miles of the border, I wouldn't have had us go there.

Ricardo says,

It's like the last moment before you die. It all happens, and you just can't believe it. A guy poked his head in and asked, are you American citizens? I think if we had said yes, he would have let us through. It was kind of random and casual. I answered that I was from Argentina.

Wayne says,

I'm dying in my seat. I was totally petrified. We're surrounded by all these military guys in broad daylight. Ricardo was so courageous. I wouldn't have done that myself. He took my hand. He said, "Could you please have some compassion. This is my family. You could choose not to do this." The border patrol officer was completely taken aback.

Ricardo remembers, "Then the guy said to me, what if I wanted to come to your country? Would you let me come there?"

The men made Ricardo step out. Wayne had to stay in the car, but could hear their voices: "You're a very muscular guy; you're not going to try anything, are you?" Ricardo notes, "They treat you like that all the time. Like you're about to burst, like you're an animal. You're not supposed to move unless you're told. "

Once inside [the detention facility], I just collapsed and started crying. They kept asking me questions. A guy there was very nasty. "You're going to try to resist us. You're going to get what you deserve. Are you on steroids? We should arrest the other guy"—Wayne—"as well."

Wayne says:

As soon as they took him, I called my attorney. An officer came out and said to me they might be arresting me, too, for transporting an illegal alien. I said that he's not an illegal alien, he's my partner. He left and then returned. "I need to ask you, do you guys have AIDS?" I said, "No, sir, I'm not HIV-positive. I'm on a work visa serving the HIV community." Then he said, "Do you understand why I'm asking that question?" I didn't know where he was going with that.

Ricardo was held in immigration detention for forty-five days.

At first, they would lock me in different cells alone. Another person who was arrested for deportation at the same time, a woman, could have her boyfriend with her, but me they kept me without Wayne, alone in a cell. They had me in a very, very cold cell for around ten hours. Finally, in the evening they took me to the detention center in El Paso.

In El Paso ... they fed us some nasty food. They took away my clothes and gave me prison clothes. There's no record of them doing that, because whenever they took a photo of me in detention, they did so with me in my civilian clothes.

The first night we didn't sleep because we were on the floor with a bright light overhead. When I got to the barracks, I slept almost for ten days. I only got up for food. People had to wake me to eat. They refused to give me vegetarian food, so I exchanged food with others. The guards would notice and try to take the food away... I didn't tell anyone that I was gay when I was in detention. You're afraid of everything. ... It felt like death.

An immense darkness. At first, I could not sleep or eat. I would wake up with nightmares, I would choke my screams, I would start crying; it was terrifying. All I could do was call Wayne on the phone. Those calls in a way would keep me alive but on the other side of the phone was Wayne, just as desperate. I went through the money I came there with so quickly because I needed a lifeline. I was in misery.

This country that I love so much was punishing me in such a terrible way. That was a feeling that I couldn't share with anyone there. They were all trying to get to the U.S., but I had a life, I was already there, and then it was all taken from me.

Wayne tells his story:

I was delirious. Back in Albuquerque, I had to change my flight. The woman at the airport didn't even need to ask; she could tell from my face...

It was forty-five days of hell. I didn't sleep. I was manic for about three weeks. They wouldn't tell us anything. My attorney was sending letters to the El Paso Detention Office. We kept offering to expedite a voluntary deportation. They declined. No explanation. It was like my insides were ripped. For the first three weeks when I was back in the apartment, a part of my mind would hear him or think he was just in the next room...

In early November we found out that he would be deported in the next ten days. I hoped to see him at his layover in Miami, but even that didn't work out.

Ricardo was sent back to Buenos Aires.

With Ricardo in Argentina, their application for partnership status in Canada had to be relaunched. Fifteen months later, it is still pending. (They cannot marry under Canadian law until both are actually on Canadian soil.) Still living on different continents, they hope that soon Ricardo will become a Canadian permanent resident and they can eventually reunite.

"I can't describe how terrible" this period has been, Wayne told us.

For six months I wasn't able to do my job. I was dealing with people with very similar issues to what I was going through. A large percent of our clients are undocumented. There wasn't a day that I wasn't breaking down and at my wits' end.

So, about six months ago, I had to resign and take a less stressful job that pays much less. I've moved from a two-bedroom apartment to a studio. The room I live in now is just piles of papers and documents. The money we spent in the last year on phone calls! We have no savings now. We're living literally paycheck to paycheck.

But Ricardo adds, "In Canada, I'll have my family together again. We had a beautiful life, and then all of a sudden, they cut your arms off. You're powerless. Everything changed overnight."

From a Human Rights Watch telephone interview with Ricardo Espíndola and Wayne Browne, December 9, 2005.

Gender Identity, Marriage, and Immigration

On April 16, 2004, William Yates, Associate Director for Operations of the U.S. Citizenship and Immigration Services (USCIS, the former INS), issued a memo on "Adjudication of Petitions and Applications Filed by or on Behalf of, or Document Requests by, Transsexual Individuals." The memo stated:

> CIS personnel shall not recognize the marriage, or intended marriage, between two individuals where one or both of the parties claims to be a transsexual, regardless of whether each individual has undergone sex reassignment surgery, or is in the process of doing so.

Yates' stated rationale was "to ensure consistency with the legislative intent reflected in the DOMA." However, in many U.S. states, as in many foreign countries, transgender people whose identity papers had been changed from their birth gender could still contract perfectly legal marriages—and had been able to do so for years. Since there is no federal family law, the U.S. has always looked to the law of the state or country where the marriage was entered into to determine its validity. The memo changed the rule, codifying that these marriages were suddenly void for immigration purposes.[131]

The memo claimed this had been an INS practice for some years. Yet one female-to-male (FTM) transgender man, Chris, wrote us that the INS "*did* approve these marriages if valid where performed, still in existence, and not solely entered into for immigration purposes. … It is one thing if you never had the right to sponsor your foreign partner for immigration purposes (same-sex couples); it's another thing if you *had* the right, and all of a sudden a new memo comes and thus legally married couples are shattered to hear from the officers that their marriage is no longer acceptable for immigration purposes!" His own story was one of rejection:

> Me and my [foreign-born] wife have been partners for eighteen years. We got married in July 2001. When I applied for adjustment of status in the fall of 2001 based on our legal marriage, the interviewing officer and his supervisor told us they will retain our application and decide if they will forward it to their marriage fraud unit or to their continuing unit—the "black hole." We were totally shocked since we didn't do anything fraudulent… Since then we're fighting. Our attorney requested more information. Finally, after almost a year, we got a note. But rather than giving us details about their mysterious claim, the note said that my application had been denied and that we have fifteen (!!) days to appeal their decision. We appealed it: that was the beginning of 2004. [132]

A year later, Chris and his wife still had received no word.

> I know more couples whose lives are shattered due to this new policy… Except for Massachusetts there is no place in the U.S. that does allow same-sex marriage, while lots of places/states do allow transsexuals to legally get married. But would the government care, or apply *logic?*—no. … As you can see it's not "homosexuals" or "activist judges" or the "ACLU" who are trying to redefine marriages. It's our own *government* who already redefined legal marriages where one spouse is a transsexual. The impact of such policy is horrendous.[133]

---

[131] U.S. Citizenship and Immigration Services, "Adjudication of Petitions and Applications Filed by or on Behalf of, or Document Requests by, Transsexual Individuals," Interoffice Memorandum, April 16, 2004, on file with Human Rights Watch..

[132] Email to Human Rights Watch from Chris (last name withheld at his request), January 21, 2005.

[133] Email to Human Rights Watch from Chris (last name withheld at his request), January 28, 2005.

In fact, less than six months after the memo, on September 21, 2004, the Board of Immigration Appeals (BIA) reversed it in a case decision. Noting that several states had allowed transgender people to marry even before DOMA was passed, while the House Conference Report on DOMA had stated that *"no state has ever permitted homosexual couples to marry,"* it concluded those marriages were not among the ones the bill intended to invalidate.[134]

Yet prejudice and discrimination still confront transgender people in immigration—and elsewhere. Crucially, not all transgender people can legally change identity, or marry. Some states do not acknowledge change of identity; in 1999, a Texas court nullified the seven-year marriage of a transsexual woman to her husband, saying that a person's legal sex is fixed at birth.[135] States that allow identity change have varying—or simply unclear—rules on what medical or other procedures permit it. The result is a crazy-quilt of local definitions and revocable rights that leaves transgender people's personhood in the U.S. federalized, fragmented, and patchwork.

---

[134] *Matter of Esperanza Martinez Widener,* Board of Immigration Appeals, September 21, 2004. While theoretically binding across the system, anecdotal information received by Immigration Equality suggests that the decision is still not widely known among immigration officers. In May 2005, furthermore, the Board of Immigration Appeals issued a precedential decision that did recognize a marriage for immigration purposes where one of the spouses was transgender. The Board found that the Immigration Service should have looked to the law of the state, North Carolina, where the marriage was entered into, and since the marriage was considered legally valid there, it was valid for immigration purposes. *Matter of Lovo-Lara ,* Board of Immigration Appeals, 2005.

[135] "Amending Birth Certificates to Reflect Your Correct Sex," Lambda Legal Defense and Education Fund, November 12, 2002, at http://www.lambdalegal.org/cgi-bin/iowa/documents/record?record=1162 (retrieved January 3, 2006).

"These are Scary Times"

Amber is a male-to-female transgender woman from the Bahamas, twenty-eight years old. While living in the U.S., she had sex reassignment surgery. She changed her name and driver's license legally. She was dating a man who was a U.S. citizen, but they had not yet decided to marry. In 2003, however, facing a deportation order, she was taken into immigration detention. Her experience showed an inflexible system unable to accommodate, or even comprehend, non-conforming gender identity and expression.

When I was at Varick Street [Immigration Detention Center] they asked me tons of questions, and they strip-searched me. They gave me two male guards even though I asked for a female guard. They responded: "Yeah, you can ask for anything but you're not going to get it. Don't worry; we're not seeing anything new."

They're rude to you, and then they walk away and make the comments. "Yeah, he looks like a bitch, but he's a dude." Relaying jokes, about trans women they had seen–"I saw a beautiful woman but then she sounds like Barry White." Then, all the young officers come to your cell to take a look… The only person I was allowed to call was an attorney, and he didn't answer. You can only make local calls, so I couldn't call family or friends in New Jersey…

Afterward they took us to Passaic County Jail in Paterson, New Jersey, and put us in a big holding pen, and I'm sitting in a room full of men. I was nervous because I'm realizing that most of these guys are convicts. You just go into survival mode; you're polite to all and you don't know how they're going to respond.

The head officer went ballistic when he saw me. "What is a female doing in here?" The officers said: "She looks female but she's not." They take you for a medical exam. You surrender your clothes and then they give you new facility clothes. I was placed in an all-male housing unit that held over eighty men; some were even sleeping on the floor.

The Jamaicans there were singing a homophobic song to me—Boom bye bye in the battyman's head. Goodbye to the gay man because we're going to shoot you in the head. Some said, "Leave the child alone." Others said, "I could just kill him." You hear these threats.

I was there for a week-and-a-half to two weeks. ... Over the course of being there, things changed a little bit... During the day, you think they want to kill you, and at night, they slip you notes telling you how much they like you.

This housing area was like a cage, an old-time zoo... At night, other cells would call me, they knew a girl was there, all day and all night —"Hey Amber, I love you, are those real titties"—you walk by and they're screaming at you, catcalling, or threats – "See you on the street and I'll kill you." ... I had asked to be put alone or in protective custody. But an officer told me that would be worse – 24-hour lockdown. Those people are not allowed to move, can't get services as readily, like law library or visits. It meant giving up too much. I was warned that if I asked for therapy for what I was going through as a trans person, they would put me in Psychiatric Watch, lights on 24 hours a day and your clothes taken away from you – anything you can hang yourself with –the jail was already freezing, all you're wearing is a little vest that covers your chest and genitals...

All this time, I had not spoken with a lawyer or judge or anyone. I had money in my account, but they never let me access it. Now, I was moved to Bergen County Jail. They processed me with the wrong name—not my former [masculine] *name, a name that was completely wrong. They told me to speak with an ombudsman about the name issue. When I protested they said, "Do you want a bed tonight or do you want to sleep on the floor?" I'd started the process at 11 a.m. and now it was 3 a.m. I told them, "Fine, I'll be OK."*

They put me in a dorm with room cells. You bunk with one person. I was bunked with a guy who did not care for me. There were tons of empty cells; I asked if I could one to myself. Next thing, I was taken to medical, examined by a nurse. I explained my situation. I was still on a low dose of estrogen and a testosterone blocker when I was at the Passaic Jail. They said, "We don't have your medical files, so we'll see on Monday."

Instead of giving me my own cell, they moved me to solitary confinement, lock-down for 23 hours a day. 75-80% of the people there are informants and sexual offenders who are at risk in the general population jail... They never let me come out for a break until late when everyone else has gone away. The phones were available from 8 a.m. until 10 p.m. They let me out after the phones shut down – midnight, 1 a.m., so I couldn't call anyone, the ombudsman, the warden, a lawyer. They said I was a security risk, and they were short-staffed, so they couldn't let me go to the law library, and so on.

Immigration officers don't come to solitary because that's not where immigration cases are. They never sorted out my name. They wouldn't send out my mail or give me mail if I used the name Amber—because they said there was no such person in this facility. My family were coming to the facility or calling the facility, and they'd be told there was no one by that name here. Finally immigration officers came and spoke to me. It wasn't until February that I finally saw an officer. He told me, "These are scary times, what with terrorism, we need to know who we're letting into the country. When things don't add up"—me transitioning— "that's a problem."

At Passaic, I was still getting my meds; at Bergen County, they told me we don't care to do that here. The story changed. First, "We need your medical records". Then the story was, "We can't treat you because immigration doesn't authorize this." Then the immigration officer authorized it, and the story became, "This facility does not care to treat this."

I didn't want to go back to the Bahamas, because I still had a male assignment on my passport, and Bahamas has strict anti-sodomy laws, and I could have been locked up. I have dual U.K. citizenship, but they refused to send me there. I was deported to the Bahamas. I was held for a day at the Bahamas airport because I look like a woman and my passport says male. They told me, "They gonna kill you out on the streets."

I'd lost about thirty pounds, my hair was falling out ... It was April and I had been missing since October, my rent not paid for months, and my job had no idea because I just didn't show up. I wrote to everyone but the Bergen County Jail didn't send it out because it was going out under the name Amber ... They were throwing letters to me out.

Soon, Amber left for Canada and got a management job there with her old company. She and her U.S. partner married there in 2005. They still live apart—he has a sixteen-year career at home he cannot afford to give up, and she is afraid to try living in the U.S. again. When she visits him she feels "a fear...always."

I do go, and every time I do go, I say a prayer before and afterwards... Here in Canada, we have no problems; we've even been approved to adopt children. It's a relief.

From Human Rights Watch/Immigration Equality telephone interviews with Amber (name changed at her request), December 27, 2005 and January 3, 2006.

Exile

Zachary, a restaurant manager, lives in New York with his French partner, Daniel, who works on an H1B visa in the fashion industry. Zachary says, "I would follow my lover to the ends of the earth. If my country decides it does not want us or our hard work and skills then we will go to a place that does …. If enough gay people moved away, well, then, the extremists can rejoice. However, we are just two people who are in love and I am not sure why there is so much fear surrounding this. … The gay community is a vibrant community which contributes so much to the common good. Why would any sane government want to be rid of that?"[136]

When U.S. citizens' foreign partners are not permitted to live with them in their country, Americans are forced to uproot themselves and leave their families, their jobs, their communities and country. Often, they turn to one of the nineteen countries with laws that allow citizens to sponsor their same-sex partners for immigration purposes.

These couples' absence is felt in the places they leave behind. Many must say goodbye to aging parents, forced to choose between their birth families and adult families—while other couples are able to stay loyal to both. Mothers and fathers must spend their final years alone or in nursing homes, even though their children want to care for them.

Partners in exile experience the ache of amputated lives. Martha McDevitt-Pugh wrote us from the Netherlands:

> I left the U.S. by choice. I saw that I could live in a country where my relationship is 100% recognized and equal with a heterosexual marriage, and that staying in the U.S. would mean having a long-distance relationship with my soul mate. I chose to leave. The option of staying without my partner was not acceptable to either of us. The idea of returning to a country where I am a second-class citizen does not appeal. It is very hard on me to be away from my family (mother, sister, brothers, nieces and nephews) in the U.S… It's very hard to know that the "land of the free" is not a place where my spouse and I can be free. My own country has turned its back on me and many other gay and lesbian citizens.[137]

---

[136] E-mail to Immigration Equality from Zachary (names changed at his request), undated, 2003.

[137] Email from Martha McDevitt-Pugh to Immigration Equality, September 23, 2003.

Some foreign partners echo the language of loss. Ayla, from Turkey, who had spent years in the United States, moved to Canada in 2005 with her American partner, Connie, because there was no way to stay together legally in the U.S. "When we got to Canada, I wanted to go back so badly, in a heartbeat," Ayla says. "I wish the U.S. would allow us to be together in the way Canada does. That country taught me a lot—a lot of good stuff, even if a lot of bad stuff. Yeah, I'm a Turkish citizen, but that was my country."[138]

Connie and Ayla in 2005 at Christmas. © 2006 Private

Exile can be wrenching not just on emotional lives, but in the practical details. Corey moved to Brazil and overstayed his visa to remain with his Brazilian partner Alber: "We have spent literally hundreds of hours in the last year and a half researching all of our options and trying to learn as much as we can about the laws of the U.S. and ways to stay together [there].... There is no way that we can."

---

[138] Human Rights Watch telephone interview with Ayla and Connie (last names withheld at their request), October 26, 2005.

> The financial burden alone of traveling back and forth every six months would be impossible. So I stayed [in Brazil]. …Words cannot describe what we have gone through emotionally, mentally, and financially. When my visa first expired here there were many days of panic and despair. We did not know how to handle the stress and the burdens and fear of what could or could not happen in the future. … On more personal levels, until we find a place where we can both live legally and together, our daily quality of life suffers immensely. … There are many things that I simply cannot do in Brazil for fear of being deported. Things like: driving, working in my own profession, flying, going to school. Every extra dime we have goes into savings for our future legal fees and potential judicial battles; therefore, even our social lives are at a minimum. … We just wish to move forward with our lives and do it together. Unfortunately, these basic freedoms are not allotted to us because we are gay men.[139]

Still, for others, liberation outweighs absence. Anji, thirty-nine, has settled in Spain with her British partner of six years, Hills, forty-two. They spent three years in an exhausting long-distance relationship after the latter was denied a student visa to the U.S. Anji says,

Anji and Hills with their goddaughter, Ellie. © 2006 Private

[139] E-mail to Immigration Equality from Corey McDaniel, undated, 2003. Brazil introduced opportunities for immigration recognition of same-sex couples in December 2003 (see Appendix B).

When I tell people I'm in exile from my country, they laugh. But it's the truth. My ticket back to the U.S. is to leave my relationship. Hills has done nothing wrong, yet she is treated as an undesirable by U.S. immigration. She wants to immigrate for a simple reason, to be with her family, me, yet these reasons don't even exist for our government.

For us personally to be in an environment that feels more progressive is inspiring. To have a country do the right thing about civil rights, to make a commitment that all people are equal, is amazing. It's a blanket policy – all people have equal rights; it's not selective. This picking and choosing in the United States leaves a bad taste in your mouth…

You can't get around the [U.S.] immigration system. We try to let people know that we didn't mess this up; we're not lazy or stupid; we tried to find an avenue to pursue, but there just isn't one. …

This experience rocked my identity as a U.S. citizen to the core. Sometime I feel like a child saying it's not fair. I feel frustrated and very ashamed that the biggest country in the western world lags so far behind on human rights on its own soil… People ask me why I'm here, and I say, because I can't live there. For the country that professes to be a peacekeeper for the world, the guardian of human rights, and the bastion of democracy, they're failing a significant percentage of their citizenship.[140]

[140] Human Rights Watch/Immigration Equality telephone interview with Anji (last names withheld at their request), , October 6, 2005.

V. "Screaming Into a Vacuum": The Consequences for Couples' Lives

Wendy and Belinda's Story (Part Two)

Wendy, who has an advanced degree in Chinese medicine, is working and supporting herself and her British partner Belinda. "But this is where I start to establish the effect this has had on me," she says.

> We live with this so constantly that we lose track of how it affects us. I am not willing to put my energy into building up a really great practice or starting up an office or establishing myself really well—because there's this sense that right when it starts to take off, we'll leave, and I will have invested all that time and energy and money into a life that I will just have to walk away from… The profound effect it has all had, on the choices I have made in my life…I'm a good doctor, and I am not using it to the fullest.
>
> Of course, there's no guarantee of anything in life. But here there's something wrong—whether you go or stay is not your decision, is at the mercy of somebody else. … I come to realize it has had a really undermining effect on how I live my life.
>
> Some people say, *Well, she has to leave, but you don't have to.* I say: *If your husband got kicked out of the country, wouldn't you go with him?* They don't recognize that whatever commitment I have is as valid and strong as theirs. If she goes, I go: we're in this together.

Belinda reflects, "We own this house. It's not a great house: we don't have money to spend on anything. We spend it on attorney's fees. Every piece of furniture has been given to us. Why spend the money when it's so impermanent?"

Wendy continues,

> We haven't had kids. I'm thirty-seven, we've been together ten years; I always wanted a family. As a little girl, I wanted to adopt children—I cottoned onto the fact there were kids out there without parents, and

> someday I could give them a home… And with all the ups and downs, the fact that every year or so we are faced with some new crisis about whether we can stay in the country—Belinda feels that to subject children to this craziness would be irresponsible. I'm not even sure we could bring them with us if we move. Some other countries, some other states in this country, won't recognize us as parents—so can we actually bring them with us? And the added trauma of moving children. Why should we uproot them?
>
> I am amazed and surprised that we are still together. We've watched a lot of couples split up because of the pressure and stress it puts on the relationship. We would be in a radically different place if we didn't have to go through this.

"All the money, the pressures, the inertia," Belinda says, "not being able to get the job you want to get, not being able to move if you want to move, not being able to have children…."

> How do we meet a crisis when it comes? Fight it, fight each other, or just go into a depressive funk? For the last three months since this hit, I have been in a depressive funk, and Wendy has been trying to help me out of it. One of us is always having to help the other through something. And so few people understand it.

Wendy elaborates:

> The truth is there's been a lot of fighting, a lot of moments when our relationship has almost split—we were so new as a couple when we had to start dealing with this that I don't think we had any established patterns for dealing with intense stress …The denial, the level of frustration, the fear, the anger—the whole big ball of it just grows and grows and it's hard not to take it out on each other. And we definitely have had times when we did take it out on each other.

Belinda concludes, "Someone said to me: a straight couple has a relationship, with all the stresses a relationship brings. Then you're a gay couple, with all the added stresses of being gay. And put on top of that being a binational couple and having no legal rights…" Wendy finishes her sentence: "You haven't got a snowball's chance in hell." [141]

Financing Love

Invisibility is not easy. The exclusion from immigration policy of lesbian, gay, and transgender foreign national partners of U.S. citizens and permanent residents affects every imaginable aspect of the couples' lives. This chapter explores the economic stresses of confronting an unjust immigration policy, and the anxiety and emotional hardship that isolation and indifference bring.

The monetary burden on binational lesbian and gay couples is severe. Partners repeatedly turn their financial lives upside down. They may go from getting by to struggling, from planning for their financial future to being unable to save—in some cases, from prosperity to poverty. When forced to live apart, their relationships are sustained through expensive trips and phone calls. To be together, they may sacrifice jobs and careers.

Binational same-sex couples stand at an intersection of inequalities: the acute disadvantages most immigrants face, and the widespread discrimination against lesbian, gay, bisexual, and transgender people. The stresses they face are inseparable from the general economic pressures on these groups.

M.V. Lee Badgett's research has countered the misconception that lesbians, gay men, and bisexuals have above average individual and household incomes.[142] Through empirical analysis of diverse, random and representative surveys, she found that:

- Lesbians, gay men, and bisexuals do not earn more than heterosexual people;[143]

---

[141] Human Rights Watch/Immigration Equality interview with Wendy Daw and Belinda Ryan, Fremont, California, January 31, 2005.

[142] M. V. Lee Badgett, "Income Inflation: The Myth of Affluence Among Gay, Lesbian, and Bisexual Americans," National Gay and Lesbian Task Force, 1998. The myth was popularized in the early nineties when the individual and household incomes of lesbians, gay men and bisexuals (transgender people were excluded) depicted in marketing surveys were widely touted. The most prominent surveys drew heavily on readership of lesbian and gay publications, as well as on mailing lists of political organizations, a mail order catalogue, a credit card company, and sign-up sheets from community events, bars, and bookstores. Despite the limitations of studies of publication subscribers or credit card holders as sources of community-wide demographic data, these marketing studies became one of the most common sources of information about lesbian and gay communities.

[143] Badgett derives her figures from multiple studies. She compares the income of gay men and heterosexual men in: the General Social Survey, in which gay men earn $26,321 and heterosexual men earn $28,312; in the 1990 Census, in which gay men earn $23,037 and heterosexual men earn $24,979; and in the Yankelovich Monitor, in which gay men earn $21,500 and heterosexual men earn $22,500. She compares the income of lesbians and

- Gay men earn less than comparable heterosexual men (17 – 28 percent less, depending on the study);
- Lesbians, gay men and bisexuals are represented throughout the economic spectrum.

The economic disparities involving sexual orientation and gender identity become even more obvious when race and ethnicity are added to the calculation. Black married opposite-sex households report an annual median income of $51,000—21 percent greater than black female same-sex households ($42,000).[144] Latino married opposite-sex households report an annual median household income of $44,420—11 percent greater than Latina same-sex households ($40,000).[145] Meanwhile, though there is no national data available on transgender people in the U.S., restricted studies indicate high unemployment, discrimination, and overall poverty. For instance, nearly a third of transgender people surveyed in Washington D.C. reported incomes below $10,000 annually[146] and 53 percent of the transgender population in San Francisco earn less than $25,000 a year.[147]

Meanwhile, immigrants are more likely to struggle financially than non-immigrants.[148] Though immigrants make up 11 percent of all U.S. residents, they constitute 14 percent of all workers and 20 percent of all low-wage workers.[149] The average low-wage immigrant

---

heterosexual women in: the General Social Survey, in which lesbians earn $15,056 and heterosexual women earn $18,341; in the 1990 Census, in which lesbians earn $17,497 and heterosexual women earn $9,038; and in the Yankelovich Monitor, in which lesbians earn $13,300 and heterosexual women earn $13,200. Her research did not investigate the situation of transgender people.

[144] Jessica Stern, "Lesbians are Women Too: A Set of Fact Sheets from the National Gay and Lesbian Task Force Policy Institute," National Gay and Lesbian Task Force, 2005, at http://www.thetaskforce.org/downloads/WHM031605.pdf (retrieved December 23, 2005).

[145] Ibid.

[146] Jessica M. Xavier, "The Washington, D.C. Transgender Needs Assessment Survey," Us Helping Us, People Into Living, Inc., and Administration for HIV/AIDS, Department of Health, Government for the District of Columbia, 2002, at www.gender.org/resources/dge/gea01011.pdf (retrieved December 23, 2005).

[147] "TransRealities: A Legal Needs Assessment of San Francisco's Transgender Communities," National Center for Lesbian Rights and the Transgender Law Center, 2002, http://www.transgenderlawcenter.org/tranny/pdfs/Trans%20Realities%20Final%20%20Final.pdf (retrieved December 23, 2005).

[148] At the same time, employment and incomes for immigrants in binational lesbian and gay couples deviate from the immigrant norm. More immigrant women in such relationships are in the workforce, partly because most women in these partnerships are *not* immigrating to be with their heterosexual families, thus earning higher incomes. By contrast, fewer immigrant men participate in the workforce, partly because men in these partnerships are *not* immigrating to participate in the labor force but for reasons such as their families. (See Appendix C for details.). However, their participation in binational same-sex relationships does not mitigate the potential vulnerability that they as immigrants face in the U.S.

[149] Randolph Capps, Michael E. Fix, Jeffrey S. Passel, Jason Ost, and Dan Perez-Lopez, "Immigrant Families and Workers: A Profile of the Low-Wage Immigrant Workforce" (Immigrant Families and Workers: Facts and

worker earned $14,400 in 2001.[150] Thirty-one percent of foreign-born full time workers earn less than $20,000 a year, compared with 17 percent of U.S.-born full time workers.[151] Seventeen percent of foreign-born workers were living below the poverty level in 2002, compared with 12 percent of U.S.-born workers. Foreign-born, non-citizen full-time workers, however, are nearly twice as likely to be below the poverty line as U.S.-born citizen workers (21 percent and 12 percent respectively).[152] Concerns about confidentiality may lead foreign born non-citizens not to report themselves, or to identify as naturalized citizens on their census form, which means that the statistical differences between U.S.-born and foreign-born full-time workers could be still greater.

The pummeling of couples' capacity to get by is steady. Debt is a constant threat. David, forty-two, spent a year living apart from his British partner, Howie, thirty-seven. In that time, they flew back and forth "about ten or eleven times to see each other," David recalls. "We spent maybe $10,000 on travel. It completely drained our finances. Each trip was at least $400-$600 in airfare. It was not something I could afford. But, even though I should have, I didn't really give it a second thought. I put it on credit cards—and I'm only now coming out of debt."[153]

David and Howie at David's mother's home in 2005. © 2006 Private

---

Perspectives, Brief No. 4), The Urban Institute, 2003, at www.urban.org/url.cfm?ID=310880 (retrieved December 23, 2005).

[150] Ibid.

[151] Luke J. Larsen, "The Foreign-Born Population in the United States: 2003," U.S. Census Bureau, 2004, at www.census.gov/prod/2004pubs/p20-551.pdf (retrieved December 23, 2005).

[152] Ibid.

[153] Human Rights Watch/Immigration Equality interview with David (last name withheld at his request), New York, October 14, 2005.

When Amy, a forty-two year old U.S. citizen, received an artist's residency in England three years ago, she fell in love with Jerry, thirty-five. To sustain their relationship when the residency ended, Amy took time off from her photography business for a second sojourn in England. When it ended, the couple clung to an intercontinental connection through phone calls and frequent trips, until Jerry managed to move to the U.S. on a two-year student visa. "It's expensive to go back and forth," Amy notes. "My career took a big hit when I was away. Jerry has no extra money because she's spending everything on school. I spend all of my money on credit card debt to pay off plane tickets." At one point, Jerry had to return to England indefinitely to renew her visa. "I couldn't get a roommate because we weren't sure when she was coming back," Amy says. "So, for three or four months, my bills doubled. I'm just coming back from that."

Amy, who earns $30,000 a year, is carrying $25,000 dollars of debt on her credit card as a result of their immigration trials.

> My goal is for us to not go any deeper into debt, which will probably mean we have to go to England. I don't think Jerry has gone into debt over school, though she can't save…I took about a $6,000 or $8,000 annual income decline. The last couple of years have just been dreadful financially. [154]

[154] Human Rights Watch and Immigration Equality telephone interview with Amy (name changed at her request), October 24, 2005.

"Financially, We've Been Devastated By This"

Callie, who has a chronic illness, hypothryroidism, and is legally blind, already lived frugally before falling in love with her British girlfriend, Stephanie, but the challenges of their situation now overwhelm her. When they met, Callie's primary income support was Social Security Disability Insurance, which paid her $252 a month. They could find no way for Stephanie to relocate legally to the U.S., so Callie is now on a student visa in England, working toward her master's degree. Callie explains that their falling in love has had a dire impact on their finances:

Talking on the phone was horribly expensive. Stephanie's phone bill was more than two hundred dollars a month! At the time, my income ranged between five hundred and sixty dollars and six hundred dollars a month. In October 2002, I started doing minimum wage work, which helped. At that time, I was going into debt. Social Security doesn't ever pay enough, so when the phone bills increased, it all went on the credit card. I probably incurred at least four thousand dollars of debt, and of course, I had no money to pay that. I had enough money to just pay my bills.

Not only did Callie have to move to England, but Stephanie too relocated to the town where Callie studied. Callie says,

We struggled quite a bit when I first got here. Financially strapped as we were, Stephanie had to move from her home, I had moved from my home; we had to move to a new place and had to finance a new home. Stephanie had to quit her job and find a new one. We moved here in September, and Stephanie couldn't find a job until November…

We live hand-to-mouth, and Stephanie doesn't even get any financial benefits. We worry that if she applied for any, it would impact my ability to qualify for a visa the next time. Because if Stephanie is my sponsor and she needs public assistance, it wouldn't look good for immigration.

Because of my school fees, I just don't have money to go home… We use the overdraft of our bank to pay the minimum balance on the credit card, and it's been like that for months now.

It's definitely put a huge financial strain. We're so worried about not taking any kind of benefit whatsoever, that we're not taking advantage of the standard ways of getting help that others just take for granted. And financial worries strain everything you do.

You fight more when you don't have any money. It's not that I love Stephanie any less, but we argue. When you don't have enough money to pay all the bills, you argue about which one you can pay, what you can cut back on.

My visa expires on October 31, 2005. But the new civil partnership bill doesn't come into effect until December 5, 2005. Again, we're packing up all of our things and getting rid of our apartment and moving again. Stephanie is moving in with her parents because we're just that broke. She'll have to quit her job here and pack up and go back to her parents' home. I'll move in with a friend in America who thankfully will let me stay there for free.

In an email to Human Rights Watch, Callie wrote, "Financially, we've been devastated by this. Between flights and international tuition fees we really have nothing." The couple now worries that Callie's disabilities and their low income will impact her admissibility to the U.K. even after they become eligible for the civil partnership bill.

Callie says, "Honestly, I feel homeless. I've moved three times in the last two years. I had no home left in America because it's gone now; the remaining things are boxed up at my mom's or were sold, all wrapped up and taken away." Stephanie adds, "You feel like you're constantly in limbo. You have no ability to make plans. You're not quite sure even about the next year." And Callie laments:

We can't even have a pet. Where will we live, what if we have to go to America, even signing up for a year-long contract for broadband internet, you don't know if you'll be here.

Stephanie says, "You're always waiting for something, you can never just *be.*"

From a Human Rights Watch/Immigration Equality telephone interview with Callie and Stephanie (names changed at their request), October 12, 2005.

Many couples are compelled to stop saving money, deplete their personal accounts, or withdraw retirement funds. Robert, a forty-nine-year-old American, is currently living with his partner, Fabian, a forty-year-old Argentinean, in Buenos Aires.[155] Robert was at the top of his pay scale before he went into exile; yet he has been unable to find comparable work in Buenos Aires. He now teaches English for a living, earning five dollars an hour. "I can't save in this situation," he explains, "and in fact, I'm still using savings. I'm trying not to go through the remaining savings that I have. I have to be very careful, but it's happening, little by little." Out of necessity, the couple rents rooms in their apartment to boarders for additional income.[156]

Nearly every person Human Rights Watch and Immigration Equality interviewed spoke of the profound impact that being in a binational same-sex couple has had on their careers. Partners who relocated, either to or from the U.S., described the difficulty of starting anew. Others told of being too preoccupied by anxiety to work at their full potential. Many recounted being forced into miserable jobs. Young people, compelled by visa juggling to start and stop jobs repeatedly, were left with resumes that misleadingly suggest unreliability. Others had to take second jobs to cover the costs of travel, phone, and legal fees. In all cases, the legal onslaught on a personal life warped professional choices.

Thomas has been living in the U.S. apart from his partner, Francois, a chemical engineer with a Ph.D., for the past two and a half years. He told us:

> It's impacted Francois' career in that he is hesitant to become deeply committed to his job because of immigration problems. It's kept him from climbing the ladder where he works. I think he also performs less than his potential because he is depressed as well. Two and a half years is a very long time.[157]

Wade Nichols, American, was living with his partner, Francis Shen, Taiwanese, in Taipei when he was accepted into a year-long graduate program in the U.S. Francis could have accompanied Wade to the U.S. legally—but would have needed to work illegally to keep their household going. Wade explains, "We talked about it, but there was the question of income. Francis said 'I could get an illegal job working in a Chinese restaurant,' and I just

---

[155] Human Rights Watch/Immigration Equality telephone interview with Fabian and Robert (last names withheld at their request), October 6, 2005.

[156] Ibid.

[157] Human Rights Watch telephone interview with Thomas (names changed at his request), October 26, 2005.

thought, here is a thirty-eight-year-old man with a master's degree, and to be with me, he would have to do so illegally? So he didn't go."[158]

On the other side, Kelly Bossi-Andresen, an American woman, described the tremendous difficulties of going into exile, even with the benefits of legal status and higher education. In Denmark, with a menial job at her partner's workplace,

> I do the cleaning, set up meetings, and make lunches. I do the traditional woman's job. It's not my preferred role. I put myself through university. I paid for that myself. I worked hard so that I can have a good life for myself and my children. To be doing this doesn't feel right to me. I'm not using all the parts of myself.
>
> When I tried to find a job, the response was, "Oh, no, your education is from the United States. We do things differently here." If you want to be a teacher, you have to study here for four years … I'm not given the same opportunities as a Dane would—because I'm a foreigner.[159]

Enrolling in school and qualifying for student visas is often the only way that foreign nationals in binational same-sex partnerships can legally stay in the U.S.; thus, education costs loom large for them. The partner cannot earn a full salary on a student visa. Yet international students often pay far more tuition than Americans students, are ineligible for federal and state financial aid, must maintain minimum savings equal to a year or more's tuition, and are stringently restricted in the hours of work-study they are allowed in a given week.

Suzanne, an Australian citizen, was a trained web developer but had to study computer science in the U.S. to be able to stay with her partner, Leslie. To remain legal, she said,

> I applied from Australia as an F1 visa student, and have to pay exorbitant course fees as well as have no legal capacity to work and offset the cost of studying here which is upwards of $30,000 US—I had to sell real estate in Australia in order to afford this; however, this was the only way I could legally join my partner in the U.S… We have been forced to put ourselves

---

[158] Human Rights Watch/Immigration Equality telephone interview with Wayne Nichols and Francis Shen, November 2, 2005.

[159] Human Rights Watch/Immigration Equality telephone interview with Gitte and Kelly Bossi-Andresen, December 20, 2005.

> into financial hardship in order to be together in the United States legally. We constantly have to be aware of every single expense we have.[160]

Simon, originally from the Philippines, was similarly on a student visa, staying to be with his partner Joe in Kentucky. Joe, he told us, is "the sole breadwinner of our family. Immigration laws are very *oppressive.* He has to work more than eighty hours a week, including odd jobs, just to be able to pay for my tuition fees and our living expenses."[161]

Other couples reiterate the insuperable difficulty of supporting a household on a single income. Betsy, a thirty-year old British woman, remains in the U.S. out of status so that she can be with Lorraine, her partner of eight years, and their two children. Because she cannot legally work, Betsy earns what she can by making and selling homemade soap at craft fairs and doing seasonal work in a friend's office. She primarily stays at home raising their children, and they survive on whatever Lorraine brings home. Lorraine's annual salary was $21,000 when they met, which had to cover not only herself and Betsy but their children's expenses. For the past two years, however, Lorraine has been back in school—which means the family survives almost exclusively on her student financial aid. Lorraine says, "I don't look at the total of the student loans; if I did, I'd drop out."[162]

For lesbian, gay, bisexual or transgender people who need public benefits such as unemployment insurance, Social Security Disability Insurance, welfare, or subsidized housing, falling in love with someone from another country can make life even more complicated. Such assistance programs make no allowances for the expenses same-sex couples (or other unmarried couples) may face. Moreover, public assistance comes laden with restrictions.

Barbara, forty-three, a U.S. citizen living in Massachusetts, is legally disabled with severe difficulty walking. She has a disabled son, seventeen, as well as a thirteen-year-old daughter. She relives heavily for physical help as well as emotional support on her British partner, Susan, who lives with her in the U.S. Barbara qualifies for subsidized housing because of her multiple disabilities. Susan is legally in the U.S. on a student visa. Yet, foreigners on student visas cannot live in subsidized housing, so Susan's presence in the house must be a secret, even though she is both Susan's primary caregiver and her partner. Barbara feels the injustice acutely: "I have neighbors who have a partner who is not

---

[160] E-mail to Immigration Equality from Suzanne (name changed at her request), undated, 2003.

[161] E-mail to Immigration Equality from Simon (last name withheld at his request," undated, 2003.

[162] Human Rights Watch/Immigration Equality telephone interview with Lorraine and Betsy (names changed at their request), November 7, 2005.

American, and they can bring their spouses, and I say, accept all; but I'm an American and I can't get my own home country to accept my own partner." [163]

Barbara and Susan in 2002 at Easter dinner. © 2006 Private

[163] Human Rights Watch/Immigration Equality interview with Barbara and Susan (last names withheld at their request), October 11, 2005.

"The Constant Fear"

Liz and Carly—not their real names—had been partners for almost four years when we spoke to them. Liz is from the Midwest—"I have an acre of land; I live in the country; and I work full time, sixty hours a week." Carly is from Jamaica. She says:

I came here really to explore a relationship with someone. Knowing the reaction to same-sex couples in Jamaica, as far as possible as I could get from there was a good choice. So I decided to come here and go to school. I got here in 2000 … and after a year and a bit I met Liz.

I was doing a master's—I finished in December 2002, and you're allowed after it to work for a year, so I applied for that. We had gotten to the state where I had decided I wanted to be to with her, but we had to figure out the logistics. We couldn't move to Jamaica, that would be a death sentence. How could we go about staying together?

We spoke to an attorney. Their suggestion was if I had a nursing degree I could get a job and an H1B visa: there is a nursing shortage. I had an MBA! I had no desire to do nursing. But I had spent months looking through the newspaper, sixty applications in one month, and there is just nothing there. So I went back to school—

Liz breaks in. "That sounds so simple. But the stress! They stuck it to us on that one, the expense of one semester of nursing school—$7,000 for three months. I was happy to pay for that but I couldn't keep that up for four years. But then they dropped the quota of H1B visas by two-thirds."

"Then I realized," Carly said, "that nursing shortage or no nursing shortage, I would never get a job. At that stage you really felt like a bullet to the head."

There is a lot of emotional turmoil involved. You are so trapped. You want to feel that you are free in a so-called free country. But going back home is not an option—it means breaking up the relationship. Here in America you feel like a rat in a cage. You can't work. You live under constant fear that you are a lawbreaker. Excessive traffic tickets can get you out. You live under constant stress that some day someone will dream up a different law and kick you out. Just the term illegal alien is not acceptable for me. I had one traffic ticket in my entire life and all of a sudden I'm potentially a criminal. Any day they can come to your house if you're illegal and put you in handcuffs and put you in jail. To go home in handcuffs—that would be the ultimate. …

Coming from Jamaica—it has a very high immigration rate to the U.S. but fortunately I came from a family that had no economic stress. I had no desire to leave—-it was almost an insult to me to leave the country. But I could not have a relationship there. I worked with many low-income families there, and I saw the desire to leave—but then to come here, not being able to work, not being able to have an income, not being able to use my two degrees—you are not even a second-class citizen, you are literally nobody. I sit there every day and wonder, is it worth this? You want to be with someone, but you think, I can't live like this, I may love you to death, but my pride won't take this.

"I don't think Carly even loosened up enough to ever start feeling at home in our own home," Liz says.

But I was ultimately convinced it was going to work out. I am fifty, I have been around the block enough times—there was no doubt in my mind that with Carly, that was it. I know I want to be with her. And I would go anywhere. I had my plans, I had my home, my house is paid for, and I was prepared to walk away from all of it, for Carly. Sometimes you just know.

"My mom," Carly says, "kept telling me all the time, 'Why don't you figure out a way to stay? Get married.' I have an aunt who lives here also; she said, 'Don't worry, I will find you a guy." In 2004, Carly entered an arranged marriage.

The person I got married to lives in New York—so I'm here, she's in Wisconsin. If you weigh complete separation versus a couple of years—we took that option. And we can visit. It was easier to swallow that pill than to leave her completely.

The hypocrisy horrifies both. "The 'sanctity of marriage,'" Carly says. "It is painful. It is a piece of paper we have." Liz interrupts. "We went to the store together and bought the ring for him. And we thought, this is all it takes. A ten-minute interview at the INS. And most of the time the officer asked Carly about real estate in the area she was living in."

"They were not interested in whether you love each other and this is a real relationship," Carly remembers. "They just want to see you turn up together with a piece of paper that says you own something together. Yet still, a committed relationship like ours, you can't get in the front door with that."

The two now live a thousand miles apart; but Carly has a work permit: "I can breathe a little bit easier," she says. "But I can't remember some things. Even good things that happened—because it was when I was so stressed, just living the constant fear, I couldn't enjoy it. Some parts of the experience, the personal stress, I have just blanked out. Days I don't want to ever relive again."

I wasn't born here, didn't grow up here, didn't have the American pride, but I had a Jamaican pride. In a country that is 90% black, you don't grow up with the same kind of prejudices. Then coming to this country, you hear it is the land of equality and acceptance; they'll accept anything. You come here and realize racism is not dead, number one. That was an eye-opener for me... I didn't fit in with black America, and I wasn't allowed to fit in with white America. And you're an immigrant. And I'm gay to boot. And you just get excluded everywhere.

"And just because we love each other!" Liz says. "That's what gets me all the time."

One thing I learned in the twelve years of solitude before I met Carly: there is nothing more important than love. And this country does not recognize me because of who I love. Meeting her when I did made it very clear that I would do anything to hang on to it. Because that's all that matters in life. The most important thing is to be with another human being.

From a Human Rights Watch interview with Liz and Carly (names changed at their request), February 10, 2005

Friends and Family

Again and again couples spoke of intense isolation. Navigating the immigration system can be agonizing; inconsistency and insecurity become constant. What a person in a binational relationship can give as a friend or family member, and what they need in return, may shift significantly. Barbara says,

> I have friends that are supportive, but a lot of them just haven't understood. Initially they asked, "Why do you bother?" In the course of trying to explain this, a lot of friends have fallen by the wayside. This

becomes the center of your life; you're not the fun friend anymore…Yeah, I'd say that probably most of my friends don't call anymore.[164]

People turn inward, Amy explains. "There's a sense of helplessness. You've got this black hole. You start talking about your life and then this major roadblock comes up."[165]

Forming new friendships can prove more difficult. Betsy told us how being undocumented meant shrinking into a deliberate, but debilitating, inconspicuousness. "I don't like to lie to people, but you do it because you have to stop the questions. When you're making friends, you don't know who you can trust: at what point do you come clean to people? And then, is the friendship real when you've started the friendship on a lie?" [166]

Likewise, partners in exile, often struggling with culture and language, can be cemented in loneliness. Wade Nichols is a "social person," he says, but in Taiwan "I have huge difficulties making friends. I have to find people who speak English, and then people who I actually like. It's hard to build a long-term friendship here. It is frustrating for me. I often have nothing else to do but come home and watch TV." [167]

Kelly Bossi-Andresen, resettled in Denmark to build her family, echoed the sense of solitude:

> Coming from a place like San Francisco to a rural farm area in southern Denmark, there's not a lot of diversity—not a lot of gay men and women here. For me that was hard. When Gitte and I had decided to have our children, and build our family, we knew that gay and lesbian culture was important to us, something we wanted to pass on to them. We wanted them to be proud of who we were, as we were, and here we are—we are the pioneers. We are the lesbians in this community. My midwife in my

---

[164] Human Rights Watch/Immigration Equality interview with Barbara and Susan (last names withheld at their request), October 11, 2005.

[165] Human Rights Watch and Immigration Equality interview with Amy (name changed at her request), October 24, 2005.

[166] Human Rights Watch/Immigration Equality telephone interview with Wendy and Betsy (last names withheld at their request), November 7, 2005.

[167] Human Rights Watch/Immigration Equality telephone interview with Wayne Nichols and Francis Shen, November 2, 2005.

pregnancy—she's a lesbian, and Gitte and I have helped her and her partner build a life here. But there's no community around us.[168]

Marta Donayre, a Brazilian national in the Bay Area, says that she and her partner Leslie Bulbuk find indifference not only from friends, but from the populations with which they identify, within which they work. "To the immigrant community, we're the gays; to the gay community, we're immigrants; and in the end, we're invisible. … I would like to stop being a wedge issue and be able to say that I'm fully a member of two communities."[169]

Couples spoke, too, of how uncertainty pervaded their lives. The impact ranges from the relatively banal, such as whether to replace a weathered couch, to the fundamental: whether to commit to a lease, have a child, keep a job, plan for retirement. Questions erode people's sense not just of where they are going, but of who they are. Thomas told us: "It makes thinking about the distant future impossible. It makes thinking about the near future next to impossible."[170]

Ashwini, twenty-three and from India, was studying in Texas where she had met her U.S. partner Rachel, twenty-eight. "My student visa will officially expire" in a year, she worried.

> There is an acute sense of uncertainty in our relationship. This uncertainty does not stem from problems inherent to human relationships, but from the laws of the land. … We are unable to make any concrete plans for our future together since everything will fall apart if I'm unable to live in this country.[171]

Will, trying to live legally in the U.S. with his partner Stefano, told us, "We always feel a sense of fear; as though someone is going to come along and say, 'You have to leave this evening.' It may not be realistic, but it's there – it keeps you awake at night."[172]

---

[168] Human Rights Watch/Immigration Equality telephone interview with Gitte and Kelly Bossi-Andresen, December 20, 2006.

[169] Human Rights Watch/Immigration Equality interview with Marta Donayre and Leslie Bulbuk, Oakland, November 11, 2005.

[170] Human Rights Watch telephone interview with Thomas (names changed at his request), October 26, 2005.

[171] E-mail to Immigration Equality from Ashwini and Rachel (last names withheld at their request), November 3, 2003.

[172] Human Rights Watch/Immigration Equality interview with Will and Stefano (names changed at their request), New York, January 19, 2005.

This atmosphere, oscillating between tentativeness and terror, does not just affect personal relationships. The Department of Motor Vehicles; the police; the bank—with no legal recognition of lesbian, gay, bisexual and transgender relationships, many couples fear that authorities such as these could frustrate their lives, or, at worst, undo them. They spoke of their need always to be protective and prepared. As Lorraine points out, "Just something as routine as a traffic stop could end our life as we know it now." Betsy, her undocumented partner, only has a British driver's license, but she drives in the U.S. as well. Getting behind the wheel is risky, but sometimes necessary. Betsy explains,

> If I don't drive, I would rely on Lorraine so much and be stuck in the house all the time. We'd also have to pay for someone to drive the kids back and forth to school. On vacation [in the U.S.], using a British license is technically legal. If a cop stopped me, I would have to make up a story that I was on vacation here and say that I was just borrowing a friend's car.
>
> But if the officer chose to investigate more deeply, she says, "You're in hot water straight away."[173]

One particularly humiliating fact for many couples trying to stay in the U.S. is that they dare not publicly celebrate their union, even in jurisdictions where the law allows it—because it might adversely affect the foreign partner's status. Rebecca and Eileen, American and British respectively, had been juggling visas for five years to remain together in Vermont. "We have spoken about having a civil union," Rebecca wrote, but

> from published information we realize that doing it would be detrimental to any attempt Eileen makes toward acquiring another visa. We fear that any action that would legally commit us would essentially put a red flag on her name—and getting temporary visas would become even more difficult.[174]

Miriam Alejandrina Morales Marin, a Uruguayan citizen, had been living undocumented in the U.S. for many years—and had become an activist for undocumented workers' rights. She met her partner, Hana Tauber, in 2002. On May 23, 2004, in Boston, Massachusetts, they married—only weeks after equality in civil marriage had become the law there. A

---

[173] Human Rights Watch/Immigration Equality telephone interview with Wendy and Betsy (last names withheld at their request), November 7, 2005.

[174] E-mail to Immigration Equality from Rebecca (last name withheld at her request), September 13, 2005.

week later, they left for Ecuador, because they knew their possibilities of being able to live together legally in the United States were slim, and their marriage only exposed Miriam's status to greater threat. "We are going through the opposite of the relationship of man and woman," Miriam says. "If I would have married a man, I would have stayed in the U.S. and gotten my papers. Only I married a woman, and that put me in more danger than I was in before."[175]

However, the ultimate victims of constant uncertainty and constrained choices are families—the multiple families that people try to sustain, belong to, and accommodate, while struggling against the indifference of immigration law. This is particularly true for couples raising children.

Children in these relationships both have a profound impact on their families and are profoundly impacted. Caring for a child in a partnership without legal recognition redoubles anxieties and intensifies strains. Abigail, a U.K. citizen and thirty-two, and her U.S. partner Lynne, thirty-four, had been living for six years in Tennessee when Abigail wrote us. Juggling visitor's visas, Abigail feared she would eventually be denied or deported: "If I am sent back, it will not only affect Lisa and I, but her children also. We are a loving family, and provide a secure and loving atmosphere for our children. I don't know how the kids would react if I had to suddenly leave!"[176]

[175] Human Rights Watch/Immigration Equality telephone interview with Miriam Alejandrina Morales Marin and Hana Tauber, May 9, 2005.

[176] E-mail to Immigration Equality from Abigail (names changed at her request), undated, 2003.

"It Puts our Kids in Jeopardy"

Steve Boullianne is a U.S. citizen, Olivier De Wulf Belgian. "Of the twelve years we have been together," Olivier told us when we interviewed them in their San Francisco home, "about eight have been full of questions."

Where are we going to live, what are we going to do? I need to wake up and know this is my bed, this is where I live. I am isolating myself from the threat now—living for today and trying not to think too far. But I know there is something ahead. There is school for the kids—Laurent starts kindergarten next year. And if we are to move, it is better to do it before he starts school than when he is in fifth or sixth grade.

Olivier and Steve had adopted two young children—Laurent, five, and Patrice, four—jointly under California law. However, they faced a crisis with the looming expiration of Olivier's work visa, due to run out in 2006. Olivier feared it would never be renewed; after September 11, he came to Homeland Security's suddenly intensified attention, because of an old and inadvertent overstay from the 1990s which had remained in government records. "Each time I leave the country, I am not sure what is going to happen," he says. "I am not sure I can re-enter without a problem."

The two considered moving to Belgium, which at first seemed entirely welcoming—it had opened marriage to same-sex couples in 2003. But then they discovered the catch—a Kafkaesque twist that meant their relationship might be safe, but their children endangered. "We could marry in Belgium," Olivier explains,

But Belgium allowed marriage with an exception: it did not allow same-sex couples to adopt. So our adoption of the kids will not be recognized in Belgium. If we took our children to Belgium, in ninety days they would become illegal there. They could be deported after that.

This was two years ago. We talked to a Belgian lawyer, and with the lawyer we met the parchet, the institution that tries to figure out how a law will be interpreted. He told us: there is no way to read the law in a way that will allow the kids to be interpreted as yours.

For Steve it is different, he is American and American law should apply. So the children would be his under American law. But Belgium could say they do not want to recognize the birth certificate because there are two men. There is a Belgian law that says that a birth certificate cannot have more than one man or more than one woman on it. If it does, it is nullified, without value. This is to ensure that adoption by gay parents should not be recognized.

Olivier is in the United States on an investor's visa, having started his own firm. In 2002, he returned to Belgium for what was supposed to be a routine renewal, but because the business had shrunk in the Bay Area's economic crisis, the U.S. consulate denied the visa on a technicality. Although it was eventually renewed, Steve remembers this as a crisis that forced them to confront their relationship's fragility:

When we were in Belgium—I guess there are a few pivotal moments in my life, but this was one—I was walking down the street and Olivier calls me from the American consulate and says, "They've revoked my visa." It didn't even hit me—I said, are we still leaving in ten days, or do we have to wait a few more days? He said, "No, revoked is revoked, they've told me I cannot get back into the United States." I hung up and said, What is this? We'd lived here years, had kids, a house, friends, jobs, an established life; and he said, "We're going to have to move to Europe." And I said, does this mean I have to go back to San Francisco and raise the kids and he visits every so often and we live apart, or does it mean I move to Brussels and start my life over? It means a lot to me. To us. And what about the kids? Maybe changing your life and moving to another place might be fun. But it's not something you want to have forced on you. Or on your kids.

"My lawyer here told me," Olivier adds, "that at the [U.S.] consulate, I could never mention that my kids were here." And Steve continues,

That's the point of the story. The reason you want to stay here—you have a family, kids, a partner—you can't describe that. All you can say is, I want to work and pay your country's taxes. Whereas if you're straight and have kids all you have to do is say you're straight and you have kids and a partner. And they support that.

Almost a year after we spoke, the catch-22 dissipated. After tense debate, Belgium's parliament narrowly voted to allow gay couples to adopt. The family still faced having to leave their U.S. life, though, because their relationship remained unacknowledged there. Steve said bitterly:

I think the last time we checked we had spent $30,000 on Olivier's visas, including flying, and the lawyers' fees, and all the court costs, just to stay together ... I would love for our family to receive the support, the simple recognition, that heterosexual couples do. Instead of having lawyers and accountants fill in the gap for us. But that's not a possibility for us now.

Olivier concludes, "It teaches hypocrisy to our kids. We tell them a lot about family, responsibility—and then we have to confront them with the reality: our marriage is not recognized here, our adoption is not recognized in Belgium; the world says differently. And the world's values are not the ones we want to teach our kids."

From a Human Rights Watch interview with Steve Boullianne and Olivier De Wulf, San Francisco, January 31, 2005.

Barbara, in Massachusetts, worried about how the uncertainty of her partner Susan's status affected her children's' well-being. Barbara's seventeen-year old son has a severe mental illness:

> It's already been five and a half years of this. At times, we think that if we're going to have to emigrate, it's almost better to get it over with. And yet: my son would be eighteen by then, but [because of his disability] he wouldn't be able to go, so I would have to choose between my partner, my country and my son. Obviously, I couldn't leave my son; he would need to be in a residential situation. I don't want to do that. It's so frustrating.
>
> Occasionally, the [kids will] hear these conversations. My daughter doesn't want to have to move, and she gets very upset, very unsure of her future, and that's not good for kids. There's been random nights of lots of tears. My daughter worries Susan will go away and not come back. You can't tell kids that it will all be okay. "Okay" to her would mean we will stay here with her friends, that everything will stay the same. And we can't tell her that, because everything might not be okay.
>
> We just want to be able to have a normal life as a family, just get past this and do what normal people do, just have the freedom to be like everyone else, and not have the government so bigoted against our rights to not have that. We'd rather spend our energy helping the kids with their homework, seeing a movie, worrying about normal financial issues, not these overwhelming questions.

Barbara, Susan and children celebrate their first Christmas together in 2000.
From left to right: Barbara's son, Shayne; Susan; Barbara; and Barbara's daughter, Jami.

Barbara underscores another tension that her family must struggle with: foreign nationals in lesbian or gay relationships often have no legal recognition that they parent their American partner's children. "It kills me that [Susan] has no legal rights to the kids. The family would be destroyed if something happened to me. She has no rights, and she can't get rights to our family because she's not an American. She wouldn't even have the right to take them out of the country if she couldn't stay here."[177]

"I think very few people can understand the dilemma of having to choose between your family and the person that you love," Thomas told us, in one of the refrains most

[177] Human Rights Watch/Immigration Equality telephone interview with Barbara and Susan (last names withheld at their request), October 11, 2005.

frequently echoed by the couples interviewed for this report.[178] Partners—American or foreign—who had gone into exile described the pain of missing family crises and family celebrations. It is not necessarily a love of place but often a love of family that keeps lesbian, gay, bisexual and transgender Americans struggling against great odds to stay in the U.S. with their partners. Conversely, many foreign nationals complained of being unable to travel—because undocumented, or because awaiting a visa's approval—which can mean going for years without seeing parents or siblings.

"Immigration laws don't just affect the individuals involved in a relationship," Ashwini said:

> Rachel's parents are in their sixties and seventies. She wants them to live with us and we want to take care of them. But how is that going to be possible if we aren't going to be in this country? If we leave this place, then her parents come along with us. Why should our families be put in a situation where they are compelled to leave their home of forty-five years?[179]

Todd and Nick had been partners for five years, but mostly living apart, when they wrote us; Todd is a U.S. citizen, Nick is Greek, and they were moving to London to make a common life. "My friends will miss me," Todd reflected, "but most of all my parents, both in their seventies, will be saddened. My mother strongly wishes that I would stay in the U.S. in order to be near them as they grow older but this would require me to abandon my partner, my adult family. I am forced by U.S. immigration law to move far away from my parents and live in another country as they grow old and need me to be near.[180]

There are significant sadnesses around not being with parents as they age, for something as minor as home maintenance or something as major as around-the-clock care. Connie, living in Canada with her Turkish partner Ayla, worried that, back in the U.S., "My mom's mentally really going down. I call her every week …She's always asking me 'When am I going to see you? When am I going to see you?' She needs twenty-four hour a day care. I try to explain, but I don't think she understands. … I just worry. I think, one week I'm going to call and she's going to have forgotten about me."[181]

---

[178] Human Rights Watch telephone interview with Thomas (names changed at his request), October 26, 2005.

[179] E-mail to Immigration Equality from Ashwini and Rachel (last names withheld at their request), November 3, 2003.

[180] E-mail to Immigration Equality from Tom and Nick (last names withheld at their request), undated, 2003.

[181] Human Rights Watch telephone interview with Ayla and Connie (last names withheld at their request), October 26, 2005.

Wendy and Belinda, faced with leaving the U.S., reflected on the losses this would entail: "It's not just us, a couple. It's about a community." [182] Tony, thirty-eight, a social worker in New York, considered the same interconnectedness as he contemplated exile with his Brazilian partner.

> Mass media and popular culture tend to think of gay men and lesbians in a vacuum. But we are so large a part of the fabric of society. We are sons, daughters, brothers, sisters. We are also tuition-paying students, tax-paying social workers, working with people with AIDS, helping people with addictions. I think you would have to ask my mother, my brother, my accountant, my clients, my colleagues, my landlord, my neighbors, my friends, my writing partner, my students, how they would be affected if I left this country.[183]

---

[182] Human Rights Watch/Immigration Equality interview with Wendy Daw and Belinda Ryan, Fremont, California, January 31, 2005.

[183] E-mail to Immigration Equality from Tony (name changed at his request), September 2, 2003.

"I Am So Scared Because of My Security"

I met Charles in Uganda, in Kampala, it was April 2002. We became friends, close friends, and after that in May, we became partners. We moved into a house together. And after that we had a problem with his job. He left there. … The landlord, I don't know how, she found out we were gay. I think someone from Charles' office may have told her. Then the landlord said she did not want a gay couple staying in her house, so we were forced to move out of the house. And then the country director of Charles' office said she wanted Charles to resign because he was gay. Charles could not find another job in Uganda. So we thought to move to the U.S.

Emmanuel was twenty-three when he spoke to us in 2005. Though he had lived in Kampala for several years, he was Rwandan.

When the genocide started I was in secondary school in Kigali. Most of my family was killed in Kigali—my father, my mother, most of my brothers and sisters. I fled to Butare and I survived. They found the person who killed my mother, and took him to jail. They wanted five people to come and testify against him, but most of the people who could testify had been killed in the genocide. They let him out. I was scared, my brother and I were scared. I went to Kampala to be safe, and I started to study English. It was there I met Charles.

Charles, his partner, is thirty-six and a U.S. citizen. They met while he was working in Uganda for a large humanitarian relief agency. When we spoke to them, the two were separated. We listened to their voices on our conference line, Charles in Washington, D.C., and Emmanuel in Rwanda. Charles remembered:

Emmanuel and I quickly became friends. I was drawn to his quiet nature, and as our relationship developed, I was amazed that he had overcome so many challenges and still seemed sane. Not only had Emmanuel been silently dealing with his sexuality, he had also lost so many people in the genocide. … Emmanuel is a wonderful person, and we have come to depend upon one another a great deal. …

Emmanuel moved in with me in December 2002. We lived together till roughly January 2004. Six months after we met the problems started. When we moved in together, the landlady got wind that Emmanuel and I were living together as partners. …

The organization asked me to resign—because they felt that my "security" would be in jeopardy in Uganda. They said if I resigned I would have a better hand in negotiating things, whereas if I didn't they didn't know what would happen. It all happened very suddenly. ... The staff were very upset, tears were shed, with the exception of the country director.

The organization knew that I was gay. I was recruited for my job, I did not apply; I did mention in the interview that I was gay and they did tell me up front that it was illegal in Uganda; "If you do get in trouble we cannot guarantee that we will be there for you." ... But down the road, ironically, when this landlady finds out we are gay and tells the organization she doesn't want us in her house, the organization construes this to mean that she could put something in the paper and that could put my security in question. There were points when Emmanuel blamed me because I had been too open with my employers.

Emmanuel and I did not go to the U.S. embassy to apply for a visa. I knew it would be all but impossible, because Emmanuel was an African male, single, unemployed, no job, no ties to the land—that he would basically be throwing money away in applying for the visa. In my two years in Uganda I have known many African nationals to apply for visas to visit the U.S., and have even written letters of invitation and reference for several, and have only known one person to be granted a visa... I'm embarrassed to tell anyone that I am American, since many Africans view the visa application process as another way for the U.S. to extort money from Africans who really don't have the money to lose.

Charles was unable to find work in either Uganda or Rwanda, and had to return to the U.S. Emmanuel could not support himself in Kampala; he was harassed for being gay. "They beat me in Uganda," he says: "I was staying with one friend, and a policeman came with another guy and beat me up. They didn't put me in jail: they just left me there."

He had to leave for Rwanda, where homosexuality also incurs hatred. At first, Emmanuel lived with his grandfather, but, he told us:

It is not safe here. I had this problem with my grandfather, because he suspects I have a relationship with Charles because of some of my friends who came to visit me in Uganda. When they came back to Kigali they are talking about me and said I am a gay, and my grandfather found out and he didn't want me to stay in his place. That's why I stay here in Kigali alone. Right now my neighbors don't know about me but I am scared if I stay here very long they will find out, and I will have a problem.

When we spoke to them, Charles was desperately trying to find a way to return to Africa and Emmanuel.

My current employer is actually considering me for a position in Nigeria. This employer does offer some benefits for same-sex couples. I latched on to the idea, thinking it will be great for Emmanuel because we will be able to be together. The policy manual said the benefits would include a plane ticket for Emmanuel to accompany me, and extra freight allowances for things that we can take—household items and so on. We do currently have staff in the field who are serving with their partners. But then I found out that one stipulation is that for Emmanuel to get those benefits he has to be living with me at the time the offer is made. We are not living together because we cannot live together; it is impossible for him to get a visa.

We aren't even talking about big-ticket items, health care and pensions—they only offer those to married heterosexual couples. We are only talking about amounts of two thousand dollars a year, and we can't even receive those. With hetero couples, if they get married while in the field, they can roll into those benefits if they live together for six months. There is no such provision for same-sex couples—because we cannot legally get married.

As the two struggled to reunite, Emmanuel, asked what he was hoping for, said,

I am so scared because of my security—what happened to me here. I just pray God that if something happens sometime I can be somewhere where I can have security, where I can be happy with my partner. I can only say that—I don't have anything else to say.

Charles, facing expatriation, spoke at greater length:

I was a Peace Corps volunteer, I served my country; I am trying to work where I could paint a better picture of the U.S. But I feel let down by the lack of understanding about what Emmanuel and I face... We've been through so much together that I can't give up now. I just hope what we're going through can help change the way other people view these things.

I feel let down by the U.S., by our elected representatives, by the people who were supposed to help me. But it has brought Emmanuel and I closer together. Not literally—but in our hearts.

(From a Human Rights Watch/Immigration Equality telephone interview with Charles and Emmanuel—not his real name—April 1, 2005.)

Health

In a situation of unhealthy strain, most partners in these couples are under great pressure—to stay healthy. Lesbian and gay foreign nationals usually do not qualify for their partner's health insurance. They either go uninsured or must find a way to afford private insurance.[184] They may forgo medical care for both routine and serious health issues—and the vicissitudes of immigration decisions cause American partners to face this dilemma as well. Wade Nichols, living in exile with his partner in Taiwan, needs knee surgery. He is reluctant to have it performed in Taiwan where, not speaking Chinese, he would be unable to communicate with medical personnel (nor is he sure his partner would be allowed to be present to help). Yet, Wade no longer has U.S. health insurance, so he cannot afford the operation at home. [185]

With the HIV ban in effect for immigrants, foreign nationals trying to stay in the U.S. constantly experience an extra edge of worry about the consequences of contracting HIV/AIDS or other communicable diseases. The same applies for many Americans in exile: as Wade explained about his journey through the Taiwanese immigration system, "You have to be in good health. I have to make sure that I don't contract any disease that would prevent me from getting residency." [186]

If one partner has a serious health concern, separation for a period as brief as a visa renewal or as long as the resolution of a major immigration issue can be a huge burden. Barbara, legally disabled, tells of the reverberations of Susan's absence when she had to return to England to renew her student visa.

> As far as daily living, I need her to lift things, to get down to the laundry room, things like that. When she was away, my daughter, who was nine years old, had to do things like carry the laundry downstairs, because I couldn't do it – she weighed just fifty pounds herself! It's not like you want your kids to have to deal with that. I couldn't get groceries. We had to stock up on everything before she left. It was a lot to ask my daughter to have to do these things.

---

[184] In addition, those binational lesbian and gay couples lucky enough to receive health insurance by virtue of U.S. domestic partnerships must pay taxes on the health insurance, since non-spousal insurance appears as added income that is taxed.

[185] Human Rights Watch telephone interview with Wade Nichols and Francis Shen, November 2, 2005.

[186] Ibid.

> I walk with a cane, but there are days when I literally can't walk. I live on the second floor, so I can't always get out. It would be really, really difficult to function without Susan. Even to lose her to change her visa is a huge hardship.[187]

Being apart, or being financially burdened by their immigration hardships, often means that couples cannot support each other in health emergencies. Before they went into exile in Spain, Anji lived in San Diego and Hills lived in London. "When Hills was diagnosed with malignant melanoma, she sat in a doctor's office alone. The diagnosis came before I could get on a plane over there."[188]

The fact or even the fear of separation from loved ones can erode or devastate a partner's health. Anxiety, depression, fear, insomnia, exhaustion, eating disorders, and even suicidal thoughts are only some ways that the experience of injustice infiltrates the most personal realms of peoples' lives: their bodies and minds.

Felipe is a Colombian geology professor who teaches at a community college in Texas. After twelve years of visa juggling, he recently became a permanent resident, but remembers a decade during which "My self-esteem was underground. Many times during my lunch break, I would just drive my car to a parking lot for half an hour and cry."[189] Ben, a San Franciscan whose German partner Kurt had to leave the country when his visa ran out, told us:

> I've had to be treated for depression since then. … It's been a tremendous amount of storm and stress about the condition of our family. We are in our eighth year together, and have a family unit just like any other couple. It's distressing to come home at night and find your lover not there. It's painful to come home and have no partner in the house, just emptiness.[190]

---

[187] Human Rights Watch telephone interview with Barbara and Susan (last names withheld at their request), October 11, 2005.

[188] Human Rights Watch/Immigration Equality telephone interview with Anji (last names withheld at their request), October 6, 2005.

[189] Human Rights Watch telephone interview with Felipe and Anthony (names changed at their request), November 5, 2005.

[190] Human Rights Watch interview with Ben and Kurt (names changed at their request), San Francisco, January 30, 2005.

Such apparently endless pressure leads some to an ominous brink. After long separation from his partner of eight years with little hope of living together in the U.S., Thomas found himself "suddenly having these thoughts that I've not had before."

> This sort of situation makes people ask themselves fundamental questions that the average person doesn't have to ask themselves… Others don't understand your struggle, or they can't do anything about it. You're left screaming into a vacuum and asking what point your individual existence has. If you're looking for answers, you won't get one. [191]

Mental and physical problems can lead to increased alcohol and drug use and dependencies. Partners told us of drinking as a "coping mechanism."[192] Kelly McGowan sees her present striving as part of a story that began with the difficulties of growing up lesbian in "an Irish-American family in a predominantly Catholic city in the 60's and 70's":

> Needless to say, I have had to work very hard since then, with lots of therapy and peer support, to create a life that is free from the emotional pain that is caused by being disenfranchised from both my family and community. Self-help has also enabled me to avoid using drugs and alcohol— a way of coping that has caused harm to too many queers—as the only way to deal with these kinds of emotions. But until the U.S. recognizes my rights to live here with my life partner, she and I will have to deal with the day-to-day struggles and related stress that comes from being an outsider. A day doesn't go by when I don't wonder what more productive things I and the rest of this country could be accomplishing if we weren't organized around these kind of battles.[193]

Indeed, some relationships cannot survive the blows. Madison, in Kentucky, wrote of her former lover from Australia:

> She and I are no longer intimate partners. The relationship lasted almost three years and we gave up after that because we couldn't find a way to be together due to lack of money and more importantly the lack of a visa. We were only able to spend about four and a half months of that time

---

[191] Human Rights Watch telephone interview with Thomas (name changed at his request), October 26, 2005.

[192] Human Rights Watch telephone interview with Thomas (names changed at his request), October 26, 2005.

[193] E-mail to Human Rights Watch from Kelly McGowan, March 3, 2006.

> physically together: and that was enough for us both to realize that we wanted to spend the rest of our lives together and someday get married.

"How could there be a rule that says two people can't love another?" Madison demands. "What difference does it make if they're the same gender?" And she adds, "Let's be realistic—I'm gay—no one knows I exist." [194]

"I Have Played by the Rules, and This is What I Get"

Jay Vega is a fifty-one-year-old Mexican-American female-to-male transgender man who was engaged to Catherine, a Canadian woman. Yet, unable legally to marry, the couple was unable legally to be together. There was no legal option for Catherine to move permanently to the U.S.; their only remaining possibility was for Jay to relocate to Canada. However, Jay's salary was more than twice Catherine's and he owned his own home, so they determined to endure a long distance relationship until Jay's retirement at fifty-five.

While the two were living in their respective countries, an opportunity arose for what would be a dream come true: to adopt a newborn baby. They planned for Catherine to care for the child in Canada and for Jay to continue working in the U.S. to support their family. But the burdens of child-rearing and supporting a family became taxing beyond their imagination. Jay explains,

I started working two jobs in April 2004. It was expensive –the phone bills and traveling back and forth to see each other was a lot of money. When we knew the baby was coming, that was even more a need for money. I refinanced my home to try to work all of this out, including paying for legal fees to be able to adopt the child.

Jay began working seventy-two hours—seven days—a week. "My only relaxation was Sundays when I got off at 3 p.m. and tried to have dinner with a friend. The second job cut my ability to travel. Catherine's taking care of the baby; I'm working two jobs; we can't see each other as often as we were." At his full-time job,

[194] E-mail to Immigration Equality from Madison (last name withheld at her request), undated, 2003.

My attention wasn't as focused as it should have been. … It created personal blocks. I just couldn't give what my employer needed. I didn't have the mental wherewithal. I couldn't do it because I might have to travel for my professional job, but I had a second job that was not flexible at all…

I started out in the projects. And I did all that stuff you're supposed to; I didn't ask for anything special … And Catherine and I didn't take a dime from either government asking for assistance…

After all this, I felt and I feel like a person without a country. My father fought in the Korean War; my brothers fought; I would have too if they would have taken me. I pay my taxes. I've never been in jail. Bill Clinton used to talk about playing by the rules. Well, I have played by the rules, and this is what I get…

The stresses on Jay and Catherine led to their breakup. When Human Rights Watch and Immigration Equality last contacted Jay, he was struggling to recover from the collapse of his family and his dream. The circumstances had proven insurmountable:

We felt very much alone. She felt like a single mom, not supported. Basically, all I could do was send checks. … I tried to be positive, but it wears you down, it takes you to the edge. I have my strengths and I have my weaknesses, but under that kind of stress, under the impossibility of our trying to be together physically, it took a toll on me, on my physical and spiritual outlook. It wore me down; it wore her down. I could provide a financial foundation and a values foundation, but other than that, I wasn't able to give so much more. I felt like the situation was completely hopeless, not her or me, just the situation of the laws.

You just need that pat on the back or that massage or just being able to look them in the eye and say, "Honey, it's going to be all right. I'll take the turn of getting up in the middle of the night; I'll feed the baby."

I wanted and dreamt all my life of the woman that was the right one for me and that I would be the right one for her. We were engaged until early this summer when we broke up. That was our relationship: she was my wife and I was her husband. At the very least, we were official fiancés. I waited for the perfect woman and the perfect time, but we weren't from the same country.

From Human Rights Watch/Immigration Equality telephone interview with Jay Vega, October 10, 2005.

Yet from all these stories, two threads emerged. First, whether as individuals or couples, against the odds, people defended the lives they had defined for themselves against the state's indifference. Kurt, looking back on his battle to stay with his partner Ben, says, "One thing I've learned about myself: it is possible to find the courage to fight back and to establish the life you want to live." [195] Second, couples insisted again and again on seeing the political as well as personal dimensions of their ordeals. One man wrote us:

> I sacrificed two years serving my country in the Peace Corps, promoting American values such as the freedom to pursue happiness. I now realize that these values do not apply to me and that I am in essence a second-class citizen… Do our elected officials enjoy tearing couples apart? Do they enjoy seeing a group of their fellow Americans suffer?[196]

Tom, in Texas, carrying on a long-distance relationship with his Vietnamese partner, Phong, said:

> I think about my father who fought many wars so that citizens of this country could remain free to choose. Now this very same country my father put his life on the line for denies me the right to choose… I do not want to leave my country but my country has already left me. I think this is a very sad day for the United States of America. For a country to turn its back on its citizens is a disgrace.[197]

---

[195] Human Rights Watch interview with Ben and Kurt (names changed at their request), San Francisco, January 30. 2005.

[196] E-mail to Immigration Equality from a man who requested anonymity, August 29, 2003.

[197] E-mail to Immigration Equality from Tom (last name withheld at his request), October 23, 2003.

VI. Law, Relationships, Families

Wendy and Belinda's Story (Part Three)

Who belongs?

A recent experience, Belinda realizes, has led her to reflect deeply on the meaning of belonging—and take a step toward political action. In February 2004, when San Francisco's mayor offered marriage licenses to same-sex couples, she and Wendy wed.

> It was amazing. I think I didn't realize how oppressed I'd been until after I got married—on so many different levels it was a validation of who I was and who I loved; it was so much more than I ever expected it to be.... You think it's just going down to an office and you have the registrar just say these words, but it was so phenomenal, it had so much meaning and depth that I never thought it would. Everyone said, *the courts are going to stop it*—but you thought at the same time, *This will lead to something, something will change*—it was just an incredible time. We thought, *we're recognized at last!*—and we were in line with two women who had driven up from Los Angeles with their little babies, who had been together for fourteen years.

Wendy continues,

> We witnessed for them and they witnessed for us, and the four of us were just a giddy wreck after. I think really truly deep inside of me I was not prepared for the idea of being married. Even though I thought in every way I was already married, the reality, the power of having it seen and recognized in that way—it was just overwhelming.
>
> The interesting thing was—for a lot of binational couples, they could not have made that choice: it would have been dangerous for them to be so open about their love. We walked down the lines afterward, looking for people who were binational couples and making sure they understood the implications of what they were doing. We were talking to the activists who were there, telling them to be on the lookout for binational couples.

The next day, Belinda called her lawyer. "I asked her about the consequences for me. She said, 'You have an H1B, that allows you an intent to stay in the country.' And marriage is an intent to stay. But this could cause problems if, for instance, I decided to go back to school, and a student visa doesn't allow you intent to stay. Especially because our picture, our story, has been very much out there."

Wendy remembers when they started to go public with their situation, and began campaigning for the UAFA.

> Belinda started going to Immigration Equality meetings. It was an outlet for her fear over possibly leaving—someplace to put it. She got more and more involved, mostly because ...she wanted to see more action. ... And I found out! And I said, *I think we should have a conversation about this!* How much jeopardy are we putting ourselves in? ... We decided we were relatively safe because of the nature of her visa—and we also realized how important it was to get a voice out there. It is safer for us than for others who just can never step in front of a camera or talk to a reporter.

Belinda adds: "If we don't stand up and get our voices out there, then no one is ever going to hear us. But it is easier for us because we feel we are speaking for them—all those thousands and thousands of stories."

"I will tell you an amazing thing," Wendy says.

> We were involved in this thing called the Marriage Caravan that went across the country, campaigning for marriage equality. And everywhere we met binational couples. In Ohio, in Pennsylvania, in Iowa—we met someone who was in a couple and the partner was abroad, people who were leaving the country— there is no way to track how many couples are in this situation and what is happening to them. I think we expected there would be these couples like us on the coasts, but they are everywhere.
>
> And I am so angry. I am an American. I am guaranteed the right to life, liberty, the pursuit of happiness. ... I was taught all my life that I could be anybody, I could solve any problem. And what I've had to come to grips with is that no matter how hard I work, no matter how creatively I search for a solution—there is none. And my government, which is

> supposed to look out for me, doesn't give a damn about it. Or about the effect on my family, my community, my life.
>
> It isn't just about immigration. It's about my right to live my life fully, to be with the partner I choose, who just happens to be from another country. And people do that every day and bring their partners over here. And I can't: because of bigotry and prejudice. … Hold me to whatever standards you want to; make me prove this relationship. I will. I will go through all the same things that any heterosexual trying to bring their spouse into the country goes through. But I'm not even allowed that opportunity.

Belinda says, "There's so many good things about this country. And yet it contradicts itself so much."

> In the U.K., they are changing marriage laws so that we can have a civil partnership that is virtually marriage but called by a different name. … It's something that's so simple to sort out. Just giving basic rights to couples. For the far right, it seems to be a big deal—but the reality is, it wouldn't affect them at all.

Wendy adds:

> It's not going to encourage a flood of couples coming into the country. They're already here! Just let them be legal; let them live sane lives without fear. Belinda has been paying taxes almost eight years—they are happy to take her money, just not her.
>
> How can we make a difference? How can we reach the hearts and minds of people who can just change the law? What do they need to actually start seeing us as people instead of problems?

"It's an American issue," Belinda says.

Wendy answers: "It's an American civil rights issue." [198]

---

[198] Human Rights Watch/Immigration Equality interview with Wendy Daw and Belinda Ryan, Fremont, California, January 31, 2005.

Legal Protections against Unequal Treatment

Non-discrimination means, in essence: *everyone belongs;* everyone is entitled to the same rights protections. It takes constitutional form in the fourteenth amendment—which guarantees the "equal protection of the laws" to all people in the U.S.'s jurisdiction.[199] The Supreme Court employed it in the landmark case of *Romer v Evans* to overturn a Colorado law that voided any protections against discrimination based on sexual orientation. The majority held:

> Central both to the idea of the rule of law and to our own Constitution's guarantee of equal protection is the principle that government and each of its parts remain open on impartial terms to all who seek its assistance. … A law declaring that in general it shall be more difficult for one group of citizens than for all others to seek aid from the government is itself a denial of equal protection of the laws in the most literal sense. "The guaranty of 'equal protection of the laws is a pledge of the protection of equal laws.'" … We must conclude that Amendment 2 classifies homosexuals not to further a proper legislative end but to make them unequal to everyone else. This Colorado cannot do. A State cannot so deem a class of persons a stranger to its laws. Amendment 2 violates the Equal Protection Clause.[200]

The case of *Lawrence v Texas* (invalidating laws against consensual homosexual conduct) was decided on grounds of "the liberty protected by the fourteenth amendment," rather than equal protection per se. However, the majority held that "Equality of treatment and the due process right to demand respect for conduct protected by the substantive guarantee of liberty are linked in important respects," observing that sodomy laws are "an invitation to subject homosexual persons to discrimination both in the public and in the private spheres."[201]

International law recognizes the rights of nations to define their immigration policies. It is nonetheless inconsistent with human rights principles for a state to frame its immigration policies in a way that denies human rights on a basis of proscribed discrimination. When a government allows such discrimination to destroy its own citizens' right to a family life, separating partners at national borders on account of their

---

[199] Technically the Equal Protection Clause directly applies only to states and not the Federal government. However, discrimination at the Federal level has been held similarly to violate the due process clause in the fifth amendment.

[200] *Romer v Evans,* Supreme Court of the United States, 517 U.S. 620 (1996).

[201] *Lawrence and Garner v Texas,* Supreme Court of the United States, 539 U.S. (2003).

sexual orientation and HIV status, it strikes intolerably at the idea of equality. The European Court of Human Rights in 1985 held that discrimination against immigrant spouses on the basis of sex was a violation of the right to family life; the European Court also recognizes sexual orientation as an unacceptable basis of discrimination.[202]

The U.N. Human Rights Committee—the authoritative body responsible for interpreting the International Covenant on Civil and Political Rights (ICCPR) and monitoring states' compliance with their Covenant obligations—notes that according to the ICCPR, while a State has the authority to expel aliens from its territory in accordance with domestic law, the State must apply the law in accordance with "such requirements under the Covenant as equality before the law (art. 26)." Furthermore, the Committee notes that "in certain circumstances, an alien may enjoy the protection of the Covenant even in relation to entry or residence, for example, when considerations of non-discrimination, prohibition of inhuman treatment and respect for family life arise."[203]

With specific bearing on the U.S. ban on entry of persons who are HIV-positive, the U.N. Commission on Human Rights, until this year the central U.N. body charged with monitoring rights violations and interpreting standards, has made clear that HIV status is categorically protected from discrimination under international human rights law. In a 1995 resolution, the Commission held "that discrimination on the basis of AIDS or HIV status, actual or presumed, is prohibited by existing international human rights standards, and that the term 'or other status' in non-discrimination provisions in international human rights texts can be interpreted to cover health status, including HIV/AIDS."[204]

International human rights law also upholds the principle of non-discrimination based on sexual orientation. The U.S. is bound by its treaty commitments. It ratified the ICCPR in 1992. In 1994, in the case of *Toonen v Australia,* the U.N. Human Rights Committee held that "sexual orientation" was a status protected under the ICCPR's equality clauses from discrimination. Specifically, it held that "the reference to 'sex' in articles 2, para. 1 and article 26 is to be taken as including sexual orientation."[205] Article 2, the first equality provision of the ICCPR, affirms:

---

[202] *Abulaziz, Cabales and Balkandali v United Kingdom*, European Court of Human Rights 471 (May 28, 1985).

[203] Human Rights Committee, General Comment 15, The Rights of Aliens Under the International Covenant on Civil and Political Rights, HRI/GEN/1/Rev.7, para. 9 and para. 5, online at http://www.unhchr.ch/tbs/doc.nsf/(Symbol)/bc561aa81bc5d86ec12563ed004aaa1b?Opendocument.

[204] U.N. Commission on Human Rights, "The Protection of Human Rights in the Context of Human Immunodeficiency Virus (HIV) and Acquired Immune Deficiency Syndrome (AIDS)," resolution 995/44, E/CN.4/1995/176.

[205] *Nicholas Toonen v Australia,* U.N. Human Rights Committee, CCPR/C/50/D/488/1992, at 8.7.

> Each State Party to the present Covenant undertakes to respect and to ensure to all individuals within its territory and subject to its jurisdiction the rights recognized in the present Covenant, without distinction of any kind …

Article 26 states:

> All persons are equal before the law and are entitled without any discrimination to the equal protection of the law. In this respect, the law shall prohibit any discrimination and guarantee to all persons equal and effective protection against discrimination on any ground such as race, colour, sex, language, religion, political or other opinion, national or social origin, property, birth or other status.

The Human Rights Committee amplified this finding specifically with regard to discrimination against same-sex couples in *Young v Australia* in 2003, dealing with denial of pension rights to a surviving same-sex partner. "In the instant case," the Committee held, "it is clear that the [plaintiff], as a same sex partner, did not have the possibility of entering into marriage." Yet this fact could not justify denying him equal treatment: "No evidence which would point to the existence of factors justifying such a distinction has been advanced. In this context, the Committee finds that the State party has violated article 26 of the Covenant by denying … a pension on the basis of his sex or sexual orientation."[206]

The European Court of Human Rights has set similar precedents against discrimination. In two 2003 cases, *L. and V. v Austria* and *S.L. v Austria*, the Court held that a differing age of consent for heterosexual and homosexual relations violated protections against discrimination in article 14 of the European Convention on Human Rights, saying that the law "embodied a predisposed bias on the part of a heterosexual majority against a homosexual minority," which could not "amount to sufficient justification for the differential treatment any more than similar negative attitudes towards those of a different race, origin or colour."[207] It also applied the principle to same-sex partnerships in the 2003 case of *Karner v Austria*. Austria's highest court had denied a gay man the right to continue occupying his deceased partner's flat, asserting this right, enjoyed by family members under Austrian law, did not apply to same-sex partners. The European

[206] *Young v Australia,* U.N. Human Rights Committee, CCPR/C/78/D/941/2000, at 10.4.

[207] *L. and V. v Austria,* 39392/98;39829/98, European Court of Human Rights 20 (January 9, 2003), at 52.

Court held that this ruling violated anti-discrimination protections in article 14 of the European Convention. Although the government claimed that excluding homosexuals aimed to protect "the family in the traditional sense," the Court held Austria could not demonstrate how the exclusion furthered that aim.[208]

The European Court has also condemned discrimination based on gender identity. In the 2003 case of *Van Kuck v Germany* (involving the right to non-discriminatory insurance coverage of sex reassignment surgery), it affirmed "the applicant's freedom to define herself as a female person, one of the most basic essentials of self-determination." It declared that "the very essence" of the European Convention on Human Rights "being respect for human dignity and human freedom, protection is given to the right of transsexuals to personal development and to physical and moral security."[209] In two important 2002 cases, *Goodwin v United Kingdom* and *I. v United Kingdom,* the court heard complaints by two transsexual women against Britain's refusal to change their legal identities and papers to match their (post-operative) genders. Offering a major victory for transgender people's rights, the Court required changes in their identity papers, holding their right to respect for their private lives—and also their right to marry—had been violated.[210]

Other European institutions have also opposed discrimination based on sexual orientation. In 1997, the European Union's founding document, the Treaty of Amsterdam, empowered the Union to "take appropriate action to combat discrimination based on sex, racial, or ethnic origin, religion or belief, disability, age or sexual orientation."[211] It was the first mention of sexual orientation in a major international treaty. In 2000, the European Union Charter of Fundamental Rights also prohibited discrimination based on sexual orientation.

The European Parliament has repeatedly condemned discrimination based on sexual orientation. In 1993, its report "On Equal Treatment of Lesbians and Gay Men in the EC" criticized the status of binational same-sex partners within the Union.

> A striking example of a restriction of the freedom of movement caused by differences between member states is the case of a male civil servant

---

[208] *Karner v Austria,* 40016/98, European Court of Human Rights 395 (July 24, 2003).

[209] *Van Kuck v Germany,* 35968/97, European Court of Human Rights 285 (June 12, 2003), at 69.

[210] *Goodwin v United Kingdom,* 28957/95, European Court of Human Rights 18 (July 11, 2002), and *I. v United Kingdom,* 25680/94, European Court of Human Rights (July 11, 2002).

[211] Treaty of Amsterdam Amending the Treaty on European Union, the Treaties Establishing the European Communities and Related Acts (E.U. Official Journal C 340, November 10, 1997), article 13.

> of the European Parliament of Belgian nationality who was transferred from Brussels to Paris. His male partner (third country resident) who had limited residential rights in Belgium did not obtain such rights at all in France. As a consequence of this, the relationship became under heavy strains and was ended.[212]

The Parliament has repeatedly urged an end to discrimination against same-sex partnerships in freedom of movement—most recently in a sweeping resolution "On Homophobia in Europe," passed on January 19, 2006, which "reiterates its request that the Commission put forward proposals guaranteeing freedom of movement for Union citizens and their family members and registered partners of either gender."[213]

The Parliamentary Assembly of the Council of Europe—a broader association of states than the European Union—has also condemned discrimination against same-sex binational couples. In a 2000 resolution on the "Situation of gays and lesbians and their partners in respect of asylum and immigration in the member states of the Council of Europe," the Assembly noted that it

> is aware that the failure of most member states to provide residence rights to the foreign partner in a binational partnership is the source of considerable suffering to many lesbian and gay couples who find themselves split up and forced to live in separate countries. It considers that immigration rules applying to couples should not differentiate between homosexual and heterosexual partnerships. Consequently, proof of partnership other than a marriage certificate should be allowed as a condition of eligibility for residence rights in the case of homosexual couples.

---

[212] "On Equal Treatment of Lesbians and Gay Men in the EC," Report by MEP Claudia Roth on behalf of the Committee on Civil Liberties and Internal Affairs, European Parliament.

[213] European Parliament Resolution, January 18, 2006, P6_TA-PROV(2006)0018, "Homophobia in Europe."

It called on member states:

- to review their policies in the field of social rights and protection of migrants in order to ensure that homosexual partnership and families are treated on the same basis as heterosexual partnerships and families;
- to take such measures as are necessary to ensure that binational lesbian and gay couples are accorded the same residence rights as bi-national heterosexual couples;
- to encourage the establishment of non-governmental organisations to help homosexual refugees, migrants and binational couples to defend their rights;
- to co-operate more closely with UNHCR and national non-governmental organisations, promote the networking of their activities, and urge them to systematically monitor the observance of the immigration and asylum rights of gays and lesbians;
- to ensure that the training of immigration officers who come into contact with asylum seekers and binational same-sex couples includes attention to the specific situation of homosexuals and their partners. [214]

The United States can also draw lessons from other countries—both near and far—which have taken stands against inequality based on sexual orientation. In the 1998 case of *Vriend v Alberta,* Canada's Supreme Court held:

> It is easy to say that everyone who is just like "us" is entitled to equality. Everyone finds it more difficult to say that those who are "different" from us in some way should have the same equality rights that we enjoy. Yet so soon as we say any … group is less deserving and unworthy of equal protection and benefit of the law all minorities and all of Canadian society are demeaned. It is so deceptively simple and so devastatingly injurious to say that those who are handicapped or of a different race, or religion, or colour or sexual orientation are less worthy. … It can never be forgotten that discrimination is the antithesis of equality and that it is the recognition of equality which will foster the dignity of every individual.[215]

---

[214] Parliamentary Assembly of the Council of Europe, Recommendation 1470 (2000), "Situation of gays and lesbians and their partners in respect of asylum and immigration in the member states of the Council of Europe."

[215] *Vriend v. Alberta,* Supreme Court of Canada, File No. 25285, at 69.

The United States can also learn from South Africa. In 1996, emerging from the abysses of apartheid, that country became the first to enshrine sexual orientation in its constitution as a status protected from discrimination. One of the earliest decisions by South Africa's Constitutional Court based on this provision guaranteed immigration rights for any citizen's permanent partner, whether of the same or opposite sex. To disregard or discount same-sex relationships for immigration purposes, the Court said, sent a message

> that gays and lesbians lack the inherent humanity to have their families and family lives in such same-sex relationships respected or protected... The impact constitutes a crass, blunt, cruel and serious invasion of their dignity.
>
> The sting of past and continuing discrimination against both gays and lesbians is the clear message that it conveys, namely, that they, whether viewed as individuals or in their same-sex relationships, do not have the inherent dignity and are not worthy of the human respect possessed by and accorded to heterosexuals and their relationships. This discrimination occurs at a deeply intimate level of human existence and relationality. It denies to gays and lesbians that which is foundational to our Constitution ... namely that all persons have the same inherent worth and dignity as human beings, whatever their other differences may be.[216]

"The Hopes and Expectations of Humanity": Law and the Forms of Family

Debates in the U.S. over how to recognize relationships tend to assume that "marriage" and "the family" have a single character that has not changed over time: the institutions have taken the same shape, the same people have always had a right to them. Expanding their legal definition to other forms of affiliation thus seems a social change of tectonic importance.

Obviously, this is untrue. Casting an eye over a world map or through the Bible is enough to show that over miles and through millennia, families take divergent configurations and have meant many things. United States law only very recently came

---

[216] *National Coalition for Gay and Lesbian Equality and others v Ministry of Home Affairs and Others*, Constitutional Court of South Africa, CCT 10/99, at 54 and 42.

to recognize in heterosexual marriage a value so universally acknowledged as to be deserved by, and protected for, all.

For generations, for example, marriages between slaves had no legal effect.[217] After slavery, state after state passed "miscegenation" laws barring interracial marriages. These enforced the segregation system; surviving into the twentieth century, they become one of many weapons in the eugenicists' arsenal—hindering the supposedly "unfit" from marrying.

Marriage also was a means of defining citizenship—and of defining certain people out. These laws were widely used to limit immigration. By the nineteenth century's end, a dozen states forbade whites to marry Asians; nine specifically targeted Filipinos. Arizona, one historian notes, "prohibited whites from marrying 'Hindus' and … Oregon prohibited whites from marrying Native Hawaiians, or Kanakas."[218] In 1907, Congress mandated that any U.S. woman marrying a foreigner who was ineligible (on racial or other grounds) for U.S. immigration be stripped of her own citizenship without trial.

In a large part of the U.S., then—not unlike apartheid South Africa[219]—a web of restrictions on marriage and relationships upheld a racially exclusive definition of national identity. In declaring marriage "a fundamental right of free men"; in stating that "the right to marry is the right to join in marriage with the person of one's choice" (as the California Supreme Court did in overturning a "miscegenation" law in 1948),[220] courts were not just confirming the legal ability to contract a partnership. They were nailing liberatory theses to the door about the character of their country, its ability to imagine an open rather than a branded and biased future. Likewise, other steps in this century toward ensuring justice in married relationships—eliminating child marriages, campaigning against domestic violence, guaranteeing the legal and economic rights of

---

[217] "It is clear that slaves have no legal capacity to assent to any contract. With the consent of their master they may marry, and their *moral* power to agree to such a contract or connection cannot be doubted; *but while in a state of slavery* it cannot produce any *civil effect,* because slaves are deprived of all civil rights. Emancipation gives to the slave his civil rights, and a contract of marriage, legal and valid by the consent of the master, and moral assent of the slave, *from the moment of freedom, although dormant during slavery*, produces all the effects which result from such contract among free persons." (Opinion of Judge Matthews, case of *Girod v Lewis,* May term, 1819; *Martin's Louisiana Reports*, vol. 6, p. 559.)

[218] Peggy Pascoe, "Why the Ugly Rhetoric Against Gay Marriage Is Familiar to this Historian of Miscegenation," *History News Network,* at http://hnn.us/articles/4708.html (retrieved December 14, 2005).

[219] Among the first steps in establishing apartheid in South Africa were banning interracial marriages (in 1949) and all interracial sex (in 1950). This paralleled similar moves in building a racial regime in Nazi Germany in the 1930s.

[220] *Perez* v. *Sharp*, Supreme Court of California, 32 Cal.2d 711, 198 P.2d 17 (1948).

both partners, and protecting the rights of the child—also guarantee that family relations will not be a private, insular exception to the public values of dignity and fairness.

A future president of the United States wrote in 1900 that "Family methods rest upon individual inequality, state methods upon individual equality. Family order rests upon tutelage, state order upon franchise."[221] Law in the succeeding century strained to erode that invidious division, and make the family a place of choice and justice. It is certainly true that "marriage is more than a contract," as some conservatives complain.[222] The way relationships are treated—whether furthering equality or fathering privilege—draws a line between inside and outside, valued and unvalued, on many levels. It not only encapsulates how power is allotted between individuals and state; it embodies a vision of how society will develop.

In 1967, in *Loving v Virginia*, the Supreme Court finally struck down laws against interracial marriage.[223] It said:

> Marriage is one of the "basic civil rights of man," fundamental to our very existence and survival. To deny this fundamental freedom on so unsupportable a basis as the racial classifications embodied in these statutes, classifications so directly subversive of the principle of equality at the heart of the Fourteenth Amendment, is surely to deprive all the State's citizens of liberty without due process of law.[224]

This affirmed the reach of the Equal Protection Clause. It also was a step in the Court's progress toward identifying a realm of intimate decision-making as a basic part of liberty. In *Lawrence v Texas,* the Court maintained:

---

[221] Woodrow Wilson, *The State: Elements of Historical and Practical Politics* (Boston: Heath & Co., 1900), p. 638.

[222] David Coolidge, "What is Marriage?" *Crisis Magazine*, July 15, 1996.

[223] The statute in question, Virginia's Racial Integrity Act of 1924, outlawing intermarriage, was itself illustrative. Virginia had been a hotbed of eugenicist pseudoscience and practice; Madison Grant, the Jeremiah of "mongrelization" (see chapter II) was consulted as the law was drawn up. The bill, requiring racial registration certificates, was clearly meant to promote racia classification across the whole population. (This also corresponded to national trends: in 1920, the U.S. Census eliminated the category of "mixed race" for the first time in seven decades, forcing people to class themselves as either "black" or "white.") The act defined a "white person" as one who "has no trace whatever of any blood other than Caucasian; but persons who have one-sixteenth or less of the blood of the American Indian and have no other non-Caucasic blood shall be deemed to be white persons." The latter exception was added because sixteen members of the Virginia legislature, who proudly claimed partial descent from Pocohontas, feared being legally leached of their whiteness by a more constricting definition. See Paul Lombardo, "Miscegenation, Eugenics and Racism: Historical Footnotes to *Loving v. Virginia," University of California Davis Law Review,* vol. 21 (1988), pp. 421-452.

[224] *Loving v. Virginia,* Supreme Court of the United States, 388 US 1 (1967).

> Liberty presumes an autonomy of self that includes freedom of thought, belief, expression, and certain intimate conduct. .... When sexuality finds overt expression in intimate conduct with another person, the conduct can be but one element in a personal bond that is more enduring. The liberty protected by the Constitution allows homosexual persons the right to make this choice.[225]

Current U.S. immigration law, bound by a restrictive concept of family relationships excluding lesbian and gay partners, denies those persons that right and that choice. This sends a devastating message to them about their dignity and worth. It sends the wrong message about U.S. society, and what it wants to become.

Increasingly, human rights law recognizes the need for inclusive respect toward the different ways human beings relate to one another and form families. Many of its documents deal with marriage and family. The Universal Declaration of Human Rights (UDHR), the foundation of the modern human rights system, says in article 16:

> 1. Men and women of full age, without any limitation due to race, nationality or religion, have the right to marry and to found a family. They are entitled to equal rights as to marriage, during marriage and at its dissolution.
> 2. Marriage shall be entered into only with the free and full consent of the intending spouses.
> 3. The family is the natural and fundamental group unit of society and is entitled to protection by society and the State.

The International Covenant on Civil and Political Rights (ICCPR) states in article 23:

> 1. The family is the natural and fundamental group unit of society and is entitled to protection by society and the State.
> 2. The right of men and women of marriageable age to marry and to found a family shall be recognized.

There is no express definition of marriage as *between* a man and woman in these instruments. The Constitutional Court of South Africa, in a decision opening full marriage rights to same-sex partners, observed that "The reference to 'men and women'" is

---

[225] *Lawrence and Garner v Texas,* Supreme Court of the United States, 539 US (2003).

> descriptive of an assumed reality, rather than prescriptive of a normative structure for all time. Its terms make it clear that the principal thrust of the instruments is to forbid child marriages, remove racial, religious, or nationality impediments to marriage, ensure that marriage is freely entered into and guarantee equal rights before, during, and after marriage.
>
> The statement … that the family is the natural and fundamental group unit in society, entitled to protection by the state, has in itself no inherently definitional implications. … Nor need it by its nature be restricted intrinsically, inexorably and forever to heterosexual family units. There is nothing in the international law instruments to suggest that the family which is the fundamental unit of society must be constituted according to any particular model. Indeed, even if the purpose of the instruments was expressly to accord protection to a certain type of family formation, this would not have implied that all other modes of establishing families should for all time lack legal protection.
>
> Indeed, rights by their nature will atrophy if frozen. As the conditions of humanity alter and as ideas of justice and equity evolve, so do concepts of rights take on new texture and meaning. The horizon of rights is as limitless as the hopes and expectations of humanity. … When the Universal Declaration was adopted, colonialism and racial discrimination were seen as natural phenomena, embodied in the laws of the so-called civilized nations, and blessed by as many religious leaders as they were denounced. ... Severe chastisement of women was tolerated by family law and international legal instruments then, but is today considered intolerable. Similarly, though many of the values of family life have remained constant, both the family and the law relating to the family have been utterly transformed.[226]

Acknowledging those changes, the European Charter of Rights and Fundamental Freedoms, in its comparable article 9, omits all reference to sex, stating, "The right to marry and the right to found a family shall be guaranteed in accordance with the national laws governing the exercise of these rights."

---

[226] *Minister of Home Affairs and Others v Fourie and Bonthuys and Others,* Constitutional Court of South Africa, CCT 10/05, at 100-102.

International human rights mechanisms have shown respect for evolving definitions of the family. The U.N. Human Rights Committee has noted that "the concept of the family may differ in some respects from State to State, and even from region to region within a State, and … it is therefore not possible to give the concept a standard definition."[227] The U.N. Committee on the Rights of the Child states: "When considering the family environment, the Convention [on the Rights of the Child] reflects different family structures arising from various cultural patterns and emerging family relationships."[228]

The UN High Commission for Refugees has recommended, in the context of refugee protection, that right to family unification include same-sex partners.

> In UNHCR's view, States should adopt a pragmatic interpretation of the family. … Families should be understood to include spouses; those in customary marriage; long-term cohabitants, including same-sex couples; and minor children until at least age eighteen.[229]

According to the UN Special Rapporteur on Violence Against Women, strict prescriptions of what families should be not only proscribe diversity but repress reality.

> Throughout the world, there exist divisions between the dominant, normative ideal of the family and the empirical realities of family forms. Whether the ideal is the nuclear family or a variation of the joint or extended family, such ideals in many cases are not wholly consistent with the realities of modern family forms …
>
> Despite such differences, however, the culturally-specific, ideologically dominant family form in any given society shapes both the norm and that which is defined as existing outside of the norm and, hence, classified as deviant. Thus, the dominant family structure--whether it is dominant in fact or merely in theory--serves as a basis against which relationships are judged. Further, it serves as the standard against which individual women are judged and, in many cases, demonized for failing

---

227 "General Comment 19: Protection of the family, the right to marriage and equality of the spouses," U.N. Human Rights Committee, HRI/GEN/1/Rev.2, at 2.

228 "Report on the Fifth Session," Committee on the Rights of the Child, UN Doc. CREC/C/24, Annex V.

229 Erika Feller, Volker Türk and Frances Nicholson, "Refugee Protection In International Law: UNHCR's Global Consultations On International Protection," United Nations High Commissioner for Refugees, 2003, p. 584.

> to ascribe to moral and legal dictates with respect to family and sexuality … Such demonization fuels and legitimates violence against women in the form of sexual harassment, rape, domestic violence, female genital mutilation, forced marriages, honour killings and other forms of femicide.[230]

The European Parliament has again and again urged inclusive understandings of family forms. In a human rights resolution in 2000, it

- Call[ed] on the Member States to guarantee one-parent families, unmarried couples and same-sex couples rights equal to those enjoyed by traditional couples and families, particularly as regards tax law, pecuniary rights and social rights;
- Note[d] with satisfaction that, in a large number of Member States, there is growing legal recognition for extramarital cohabitation, irrespective of gender; call[ed] on the Member States that have not yet done so to amend their legislation in order to recognise registered same-sex partnerships and guarantee they enjoy the same rights and obligations as exist for different-sex couples; call[ed] on the Member States in which such legal recognition does not yet exist to amend their laws to recognise legally extramarital cohabitation irrespective of gender; consider[ed] therefore that rapid progress should be made in achieving mutual recognition of the different legal forms of cohabitation in the EU as well as legal marriage between persons of the same sex. [231]

More recently, in 2003, the Parliament recommended "that the Member States more generally recognise non-marital relationships, both heterosexual and homosexual, and confer the same rights on partners in these relationships as on those who are married, *inter alia by taking the necessary steps to enable couples to exercise freedom of movement within the Union.*"[232]

---

[230] U.N. Commission on Human Rights, "Report of the Special Rapporteur on violence against women, its causes and consequences," E/CN.4/1999/68, March 10, 1999, at 8-9.

[231] European Parliament Resolution A5-0050/2000, "Resolution on respect for human rights in the European Union (1998-1999)" (March 16, 2000).

[232] European Parliament Resolution A5-0281/2003, "Resolution on the situation as regards fundamental rights in the European Union (2002)" (September 4, 2003), emphasis added.

For some families, the form they want recognition to take is very clear. Anji told us,

> If we were able to marry federally in the U.S., we would gain the more than one thousand rights that come with marriage.[233] Rights that would give us a choice about how our family thrives and survives—Social Security, tax benefits, to adopt children if we chose. So many of the benefits that married heterosexual couples take for granted. It would make our life easier. It would give us peace of mind that we are protected and are protecting each other. It would give us a level of equality that anyone who feels disenfranchised craves in their soul.[234]

Not every binational same-sex couple, though, wants to marry. Most want the simple dignity of being allowed to be together, however that might be done or defined. The discrimination separating them is severe; a remedy is urgent. The Uniting American Families Act (described in detail in Appendix A) offers such a response. Its effects end after crossing customs. It will not answer the craving for equality such couples will experience once in the U.S., staring down possible injustices in hiring, in job benefits, in health care, in housing. It will, though, be a step—toward taking the blinders off, toward seeing the diversity of ways humans can relate to each other, and their common need for protection by the law.

People we interviewed for this report repeated that not just couples' lives but a community's values stood at a crossroads. Ben, reflecting on his forced separation from his partner, told us: "This country is going in the wrong direction, and gays are like the canaries in the mine. The ability of the culture to accept, to embrace a group like gays is a bellwether of their ability to accept change and difference in other areas as well."

His German partner, Kurt, who had lived in the U.S. for six years, added, "I still love the people. I still love the place. But I feel disenchanted. This government has this idea of being on a crusade against this minority group. For me, when I think of America, it's like being an abandoned child."[235]

---

[233] In a 1997 study requested by Republican member of Congress Henry Hyde, the General Accounting Office identified 1049 federal laws in which marital status was a factor creating differential treatment: see "GAO/OGC-97-16 Defense of Marriage Act" at http://www.gao.gov/archive/1997/og97016.pdf (retrieved November 12, 2005).

[234] Human Rights Watch/Immigration Equality telephone interview with Anji (last names withheld at their request), October 6, 2005.

[235] Human Rights Watch interview with Ben and Kurt (names changed at their request), San Francisco, January 30, 2005.

The South African Constitutional Court has eloquently limned how defining family defines a society:

> What is at stake… is how to respond to legal arrangements of great social significance under which same-sex couples are made to feel like outsiders who do not fully belong in the universe of equals. …
>
> A democratic, universalistic, caring and aspirationally egalitarian society embraces everyone and accepts people for who they are. To penalise people for being who and what they are is profoundly disrespectful of the human personality and violatory of equality. Equality means equal concern and respect across difference. It does not presuppose the elimination or suppression of difference. Respect for human rights requires the affirmation of self, not the denial of self. Equality therefore does not imply a leveling or homogenization of behaviour or extolling one form as supreme, and another as inferior, but an acknowledgement and acceptance of difference. At the very least, it affirms that difference should not be the basis for exclusion, marginalization, and stigma. At best, it celebrates the vitality that difference brings to any society. … The acknowledgement and acceptance of difference is particularly important in our country where for centuries group membership based on supposed biological characteristics such as skin colour has been the express basis of advantage and disadvantage. South Africans come in all shapes and sizes. The development of an active rather than a purely formal sense of enjoying a common citizenship depends on recognizing and accepting people with all their differences, as they are… Accordingly, what is at stake is not simply a question of removing an injustice experienced by a particular section of the community. At issue is a need to affirm the very character of our society as one based on tolerance and mutual respect.[236]

Liz, with her Jamaican partner Carly, put that in simpler but more heartfelt words when she wrote to us:

---

[236] *Minister of Home Affairs and Others v Fourie and Bonthuys and Others,* Constitutional Court of South Africa, CCT 10/05, at 61 and 60.

> We are in love. This country needs more love. Why my country fights so hard to interfere with my right to pursue happiness and live in peace and harmony with all is beyond me. It saddens me deeply. Recognizing our relationships would only strengthen our nation.[237]

[237] E-mail to Immigration Equality from Liz (names changed at her request), October 18, 2003.

Appendix A: The Uniting American Families Act

The Uniting American Families Act, H.R. 3006 (UAFA, formerly known as the Permanent Partners Immigration Act or PPIA) would, if passed, let U.S. citizens and lawful permanent residents in binational same-sex relationships sponsor their foreign-born partners for immigration to the U.S.

As the PPIA, the bill was first introduced in February 2000 by Congressman Jerrold Nadler (D-NY). It gained fifty-nine cosponsors in its first year in the House of Representatives. In 2003, Senator Patrick Leahy (D-VT) brought companion legislation before the Senate. "Our immigration laws treat gays and lesbians in committed relationships as second-class citizens, and that needs to change," said Leahy. "This bill would add America to the growing list of nations that extend immigration benefits to same-sex couples. It is the right thing to do."

The UAFA was introduced in the current (109th) Congress on June 21, 2005. It has 104 cosponsors from both houses.

The UAFA would fulfill the promise of family unification in the U.S. immigration system by extending eligibility to the foreign-born partners of U.S. citizens and lawful permanent residents. It would add the term "permanent partner" to sections of the Immigration and Nationality Act (INA) where "spouse" now appears. Thus, a U.S. citizen or permanent resident could sponsor their permanent partner for immigration to the country, just as they can now sponsor such family members as siblings, children, or husbands and wives. One would qualify as the permanent partner of a U.S. citizen or lawful permanent resident if, among other things, one is:

- At least eighteen years of age;
- In an intimate relationship with the sponsoring adult U.S. citizen or legal permanent resident, in which both parties intend a lifelong commitment;
- Financially interdependent with that person;
- Not married or in a permanent partnership with anyone other than that person; and
- Unable to contract with that person a marriage that is recognized under the INA.

A permanent partnership is not marriage and would not affect the federal definition of marriage. A successful application would confer no benefits other than immigration status for the foreign national.

Because all binational lesbian and gay relationships would be subject to the same scrutiny that eligible heterosexual relationships currently face, the UAFA would not increase the possibility for immigration fraud through fake "partnerships." The Department of Homeland Security (DHS) will apply the same standards that it applies to marriages in determining whether a permanent partnership is genuine. Permanent partners, like married couples, would be required to prove emotional and financial commitment through (for instance) jointly owned property; shared child custody; joint bank accounts; joint credit cards; shared insurance policies; evidence of a commitment ceremony; or photographs of shared vacations and holidays with extended family. Applicants for permanent partnership benefits would face the same rigorous "green card" interview as married couples. If the interviewer suspects fraud, the partners would be subject to a second, still more rigorous interview in which they are questioned separately to determine whether the answers are consistent.

Moreover, as with any family-based petition, the sponsor must submit an Affidavit of Support on behalf of the partner. The Affidavit of Support is a binding contract that lets the government sue if the immigrant accesses means-based benefits before working for a set period of time, generally ten years, or becoming a U.S. citizen. Finally, like married couples, partners who have been together for two years or less are only eligible to apply for conditional residence. This requires an additional interview with immigration officials at the end of the two-year conditional status to show that the couple is still together. Conditional residency also deters fraud.

The UAFA would actually decrease marriage fraud by removing the reason for foreign partners of U.S. citizens to enter sham marriages—often exploitative and degrading—so that they can remain with their real partner in this country. It would discourage unlawful presence, and let people live open, honest lives. For otherwise law-abiding LGBT people running out of legal options, their relationships would no longer lead to choices no one should have to make.

Supporters of the UAFA include:

- Immigration Equality
- Human Rights Watch

- Amnesty International
- Human Rights Campaign
- American Immigration Lawyers Association
- Mexican American Legal Defense and Educational Fund
- National Immigration Forum
- Legal Momentum
- National Asian Pacific American Legal Consortium
- People for the American Way

A list of current Congressional cosponsors (and the dates of their sponsorship) of the UAFA follows.

HOUSE COSPONSORS (94), ALPHABETICAL

Rep Abercrombie, Neil [HI-1] - 6/21/2005

Rep Allen, Thomas H. [ME-1] - 6/21/2005

Rep Andrews, Robert E. [NJ-1] - 6/21/2005

Rep Baird, Brian [WA-3] - 7/26/2005

Rep Baldwin, Tammy [WI-2] - 6/21/2005

Rep Berkley, Shelley [NV-1] - 6/21/2005

Rep Berman, Howard L. [CA-28] - 6/21/2005

Rep Blumenauer, Earl [OR-3] - 6/29/2005

Rep Brown, Corrine [FL-3] - 6/21/2005

Rep Brown, Sherrod [OH-13] - 6/21/2005

Rep Capps, Lois [CA-23] - 6/21/2005

Rep Capuano, Michael E. [MA-8] - 6/21/2005

Rep Clay, Wm. Lacy [MO-1] - 6/29/2005

Rep Crowley, Joseph [NY-7] - 6/21/2005

Rep Davis, Susan A. [CA-53] - 9/28/2005

Rep DeGette, Diana [CO-1] - 7/26/2005

Rep Delahunt, William D. [MA-10] - 6/21/2005

Rep DeLauro, Rosa L. [CT-3] - 6/29/2005

Rep Doyle, Michael F. [PA-14] - 2/8/2006

Rep Emanuel, Rahm [IL-5] - 7/26/2005

Rep Engel, Eliot L. [NY-17] - 6/21/2005

Rep Eshoo, Anna G. [CA-14] - 6/21/2005

Rep Farr, Sam [CA-17] - 6/21/2005

Rep Fattah, Chaka [PA-2] - 11/10/2005

Rep Filner, Bob [CA-51] - 6/21/2005

Rep Frank, Barney [MA-4] - 6/21/2005

Rep Gonzalez, Charles A. [TX-20] - 6/21/2005

Rep Green, Al [TX-9] - 3/8/2006

Rep Grijalva, Raul M. [AZ-7] - 9/28/2005

Rep Gutierrez, Luis V. [IL-4] - 6/21/2005

Rep Harman, Jane [CA-36] - 6/21/2005

Rep Hastings, Alcee L. [FL-23] - 7/26/2005

Rep Hinchey, Maurice D. [NY-22] - 6/29/2005

Rep Holt, Rush D. [NJ-12] - 6/21/2005

Rep Honda, Michael M. [CA-15] - 6/21/2005

Rep Hoyer, Steny H. [MD-5] - 12/22/2005

Rep Inslee, Jay [WA-1] - 6/21/2005

Rep Jackson, Jesse L., Jr. [IL-2] - 7/28/2005

Rep Jones, Stephanie Tubbs [OH-11] - 6/21/2005

Rep Kennedy, Patrick J. [RI-1] - 9/28/2005

Rep Kolbe, Jim [AZ-8] - 6/21/2005

Rep Kucinich, Dennis J. [OH-10] - 6/21/2005

Rep Langevin, James R. [RI-2] - 7/26/2005

Rep Lantos, Tom [CA-12] - 6/21/2005

Rep Larson, John B. [CT-1] - 7/26/2005

Rep Lee, Barbara [CA-9] - 6/21/2005

Rep Levin, Sander M. [MI-12] - 6/29/2005

Rep Lewis, John [GA-5] – 6/21/2005

Rep Lofgren, Zoe [CA-16] - 7/26/2005

Rep Lowey, Nita M. [NY-18] - 6/21/2005

Rep Markey, Edward J. [MA-7] - 7/26/2005

Rep Matsui, Doris O. [CA-5] - 11/18/2005

Rep McCarthy, Carolyn [NY-4] - 11/18/2005

Rep McCollum, Betty [MN-4] - 11/3/2005

Rep McDermott, Jim [WA-7] - 6/21/2005

Rep McGovern, James P. [MA-3] - 2/8/2006

Rep McNulty, Michael R. [NY-21] - 6/21/2005

Rep Meek, Kendrick B. [FL-17] - 6/21/2005

Rep Menendez, Robert [NJ-13] - 6/21/2005

Rep Michaud, Michael H. [ME-2] - 6/21/2005

Rep Miller, Brad [NC-13] - 9/28/2005

Rep Miller, George [CA-7] - 6/21/2005

Rep Moore, Dennis [KS-3] - 6/21/2005

Rep Moore, Gwen [WI-4] - 12/22/2005

Rep Moran, James P. [VA-8] - 6/21/2005

Rep Napolitano, Grace F. [CA-38] - 6/21/2005

Rep Neal, Richard E. [MA-2] - 7/26/2005

Rep Olver, John W. [MA-1] - 6/29/2005

Rep Owens, Major R. [NY-11] - 6/29/2005

Rep Pallone, Frank, Jr. [NJ-6] - 6/21/2005

Rep Pastor, Ed [AZ-4] - 6/21/2005

Rep Payne, Donald M. [NJ-10] - 6/21/2005

Rep Pelosi, Nancy [CA-8] - 7/28/2005

Rep Rangel, Charles B. [NY-15] - 6/21/2005

Rep Rothman, Steven R. [NJ-9] - 6/21/2005

Rep Sabo, Martin Olav [MN-5] - 6/21/2005

Rep Sanchez, Linda T. [CA-39] - 6/21/2005

Rep Sanders, Bernard [VT] - 6/21/2005

Rep Schakowsky, Janice D. [IL-9] - 6/21/2005

Rep Schiff, Adam B. [CA-29] - 6/29/2005

Rep Serrano, Jose E. [NY-16] - 6/21/2005

Rep Sherman, Brad [CA-27] - 6/21/2005

Rep Simmons, Rob [CT-2] - 6/21/2005

Rep Smith, Adam [WA-9] - 6/21/2005

Rep Solis, Hilda L. [CA-32] - 6/29/2005

Rep Stark, Fortney Pete [CA-13] - 6/21/2005

Rep Tierney, John F. [MA-6] - 6/21/2005

Rep Wasserman Schultz, Debbie [FL-20] 11/18/2005

Rep Watson, Diane E. [CA-33] - 7/26/2005

Rep Waxman, Henry A. [CA-30] - 6/21/2005

Rep Weiner, Anthony D. [NY-9] - 6/21/2005

Rep Wexler, Robert [FL-19] - 11/10/2005

Rep Woolsey, Lynn C. [CA-6] - 6/21/2005

Rep Wu, David [OR-1] - 7/26/2005

SENATE COSPONSORS (10), ALPHABETICAL:

Sen Boxer, Barbara - 6/21/2005 [CA]

Sen Chafee, Lincoln - 6/21/2005 [RI]

Sen Corzine, Jon S. - 6/21/2005 [NJ]

Sen Dayton, Mark - 6/21/2005 [MN]

Sen Feingold, Russell D. - 6/21/2005 [WI]

Sen Jeffords, James M. - 6/21/2005 [VT]

Sen Kennedy, Edward M. - 6/21/2005 [MA]

Sen Kerry, John F. - 10/31/2005 [MA]

Sen Lautenberg, Frank R. - 6/21/2005 [NJ]

Sen Murray, Patty- 6/21/2005 [WA]

Appendix B: Countries Protecting Same-Sex Couples' Immigration Rights

Human Rights Watch and Immigration Equality have identified nineteen[238] countries that recognize lesbian and gay relationships for immigration purposes. This appendix outlines how they do so.

The forms of such recognition are diverse; they belie the argument that acknowledging same-sex partnerships in the immigration system is necessarily a first step toward equality in civil marriage.

- Some countries—such as South Africa or Spain—have indeed revised their immigration policies in the process of instituting marriage equality.
- Some—such as Germany or the Scandinavian nations—have created a special legal status for lesbian and gay partnerships and recognized that status in immigration.
- Some—like France or New Zealand—have created a special status different from marriage which is open to both same-sex and different-sex couples and recognized that status in immigration.
- Some—like Portugal—have opened an existing legal status different from marriage (such as common-law marriage or *concubinage*) to same-sex couples, and recognized that status in immigration.
- Still others—such as Israel or Brazil—have recognized same-sex relationships in the immigration system alone, without giving them broader status in national law.

In rare instances, the change has been mandated by the courts. More often, a legislative majority mandated it—or even, as in Switzerland, a national referendum. In some cases, immigration authorities themselves brought about policy reform.

For the most part, these changes have been uncontroversial—even in places like Australia, where anti-immigrant sentiment runs strong. Reports do not indicate floods of new applicants or increasing fraud. What these national experiences do suggest is an

---

[238] In addition, Ireland is now considering a civil partnership bill which would also give immigration recognition to same-sex partners: Civil Partnership Bill 2004, at http://www.oireachtas.ie/documents/bills28/bills/2004/5404/b5404s.pdf (retrieved December 18, 2005).

increased and necessary sensitivity to the diversity of human relationships and families.[239] Expanding existing categories, and developing new ones, both answer the felt need for an extended and nuanced legal vocabulary to describe those families.[240]

Australia

Since 1995, Australia has provided immigration rights to binational same-sex couples through an "interdependency visa."[241] This allows residency to a foreign national in a lesbian or gay relationship with an Australian citizen or permanent resident (or eligible New Zealand citizen[242]). An interdependent relationship is one "in which a couple have a mutual commitment to a shared life to the exclusion of all others. The relationship between them is genuine and continuing, and they live together, or do not live separately and apart on a permanent basis. This is usually a same-sex partner relationship."[243] To be eligible for an interdependency visa, one must:

---

[239] It is also true, however, that from the welter of categories comes confusion. States which do not extend full marriage rights, but recognize other legal statuses into which same-sex couples can enter, place differing definitions and criteria on "civil partnerships," "registered partnerships," or "*de facto* unions." Some can be formalized by a civil ceremony; some require proofs of extended cohabitation which are not required of heterosexual married couples. As a result, states may not recognize legally valid partnerships acknowledged or concluded elsewhere. (Even the Scandinavian countries, which have closely comparable versions of registered partnership, only achieved cross-recognition through a special treaty.) Britain, for example, honors civil partnerships or marriage legally formalized by same-sex couples elsewhere, as comparable to their own recognition of such relationships; Britain even offers a roster of jurisdictions whose solemnities it will accept—and Portugal, which recognizes same-sex relationships as unceremonialized common-law unions, is not on it. A Portuguese-recognized union might be accepted for British immigration purposes on a discretionary basis (and a British citizen's Portuguese partner could in any case gain entry to the U.K. under the equivalent of a fiance/e visa to conclude a civil partnership); but it is not clear whether a U.K. partnership would be recognized by Portugal, as a substitute for its own immigration requirement that partners must have cohabited for two years.

[240] An especially thoughtful discussion of this need can be found in the Law Commission of Canada's report *Beyond Conjugality: Recognizing and Supporting Personal Adult Relationships* (2001), which argues that "governments have tended to rely too heavily on conjugal relationships in accomplishing what are otherwise important state objectives. Focusing only on spousal or conjugal relationships is simply not the best way to promote the state's interests in close personal relationships since it excludes other relationships that are also important. But, instead of simply arguing that some relationships that are currently excluded (such as non-conjugal relationships) should be included, the Law Commission is of the view that it is time for governments to re-evaluate the way in which personal adult relationships are regulated." Online at http://www.lcc.gc.ca/en/themes/pr/cpra/report.asp.

[241] The visa was actually created by an Immigration Ministry change to the Migration Regulations in 1991, but its use by lesbian and gay couples was not made explicit until 1995. See "Gay Migration Rules Are Eased" at http://www.qrd.org/qrd/world/immigration/au-qi (retrieved January 25, 2006).

[242] The 1973 Trans-Tasman Travel Arrangement allows New Zealand and Australian citizens to visit, live, and work in one another's countries.

[243] Australian Government Department of Immigration and Multicultural and Indigenous Affairs, *Partner Migration Booklet,* 2005, p. 4, online at http://www.immi.gov.au/allforms/booklets/1127.pdf (retrieved January 4, 2006).

- Be sponsored by a partner who is citizen or permanent resident;
- Be at least eighteen;
- Not be a close relative;
- Demonstrate a "genuine and continuing" relationship;
- Show the partners have been in an interdependent relationship for at least twelve months;
- Show they are living together or only temporarily separated;
- Meet health and character requirements.[244]

The foreign partner applies for a temporary and permanent visa at the same time. The temporary independency visa is granted if all criteria are met; it also allows a work permit. Two years later, the permanent interdependency visa application is decided. If the couple has already been living together for five years or more, a permanent visa may be granted immediately; if the couple has a dependent child, the waiting period may be reduced.

This effectively grants lesbian and gay couples the same immigration rights Australia extends to *"de facto"* couples—that is, heterosexual common-law spouses (who apply under a "spousal visa"). Heterosexual married couples also apply for a spousal visa, but they do not have to show a twelve-month relationship to receive it.[245]

Belgium

Belgium has recognized same-sex relationships for immigration purposes since 1997. A partner in a "stable relationship" with a person residing legally in Belgium may apply for a Type D visa, which allows an extended (longer than ninety days) stay in the country. The application procedure is identical for same-sex and opposite-sex relationships. The foreign partner must present:

---

[244] Ibid., pp. 34-39. Tuberculosis is a reason for health exclusion, but not HIV.

[245] However, Australia does not recognize same-sex marriages performed in countries where they are legal. In early 2006, the government blocked an Australian citizen's attempt to marry his Austrian partner in the Netherlands, by refusing to issue a certificate that he was not already married, required by Dutch law. The embassy told him that "Following the advice of the Australian Attorney-General's Department … Australian law does not allow the issue of a Certificate of No Impediment to Marriage to persons wishing to enter into a same-sex marriage." "Govt defends block to same sex marriage," *The Age* (Australia), January 18, 2006.

- Proof that the other partner is a lawful Belgian resident or citizen;
- Documents proving that neither of the parties is married to someone else;
- A birth certificate;
- Evidence of the stability of the relationship;
- Evidence that the partner living in Belgium has sufficient means of support;
- A declaration of financial responsibility for the cohabiting partner signed by the partner living in Belgium;
- A certificate of good conduct;
- A medical certificate.[246]

Belgium recognizes marriages and partnerships legally performed in other countries and valid at the national level there. Persons in such partnerships are eligible for a Family Members/Unification Visa and must submit:

- A certified copy of the marriage or partnership certificate;
- A recent certificate of good conduct;
- Evidence that the spouse is a legal resident of Belgium.[247]

In 2003, Belgium became the second country in the contemporary world, after the Netherlands, to extend legal marriage to same-sex couples. Originally, this was only available to binational couples if the non-Belgian partner came from a country that also recognized such marriages. However, the law was later changed to allow any same-sex couple to marry in Belgium so long as one of the spouses had lived there for three months.[248] This opened new immigration alternatives:

- A Belgian national or resident may bring a same-sex spouse into Belgium under provisions allowing family members of foreign nationality to immigrate.[249]
- A foreign national can apply for a Type C visa, or "Visa With a View to Marry," which allows entry after certifying the Belgian national or resident's intent to marry them.[250]

---

[246] See http://www.diplomatie.be/en/travel/visaLangdetail.asp?TEXTID=22047 (retrieved January 10, 2006).

[247] Ibid.

[248] See "Belgium Offers Legal Marriage," Partners Task Force for Gay and Lesbian Couples, at http://buddybuddy.com/mar-belg.html (retrieved December 12, 2005).

[249] See http://www.diplomatie.be/en/travel/visaLangdetail.asp?TEXTID=22019 (retrieved January 27, 2006).

Brazil

Brazil offers no comprehensive national-level legal acknowledgement of lesbian and gay relationships—though the federal government does recognize such partners' rights to inherit each other's pension and social security benefits, and several local jurisdictions have passed domestic-partnership laws. However, a December 3, 2003 decree by the National Immigration Council allows temporary or permanent visas to be given to same-sex partners of Brazilian citizens who have any of the following:

- A "certificate of concubinage" issued by a governmental office in Brazil or abroad;
- Proof of "stable partnership issued by a Family Court Judge or corresponding authority in Brazil or abroad";
- Proof of mutual dependency issued by a government body in Brazil or abroad;
- Certification "or similar document, issued by a civil registry authority or the equivalent abroad, of cohabitation for more than five consecutive years";
- Proof of "a common dependent child."[251]

In effect, this means that couples with children and couples who have legally formalized their partnership anywhere—including a city or county registry, within or outside Brazil—can enjoy immigration rights similar to married couples. Same-sex couples unable to meet these criteria, like unmarried opposite-sex couples, can apply for a so-called "concubine visa," granted on a discretionary basis.

Canada

Canada provides extremely broad immigration rights to lesbian and gay couples through three instruments: the Immigration and Refugee Protection Act;[252] the corresponding Immigration and Refugee Protection Regulations;[253] and—most recently —the Civil

---

[250] See http://www.diplomatie.be/en/travel/visaLangdetail.asp?TEXTID=22047 (retrieved January 27, 2006).

[251] Ministry of Work and Employment, National Immigration Council, "Administrative Resolution No. 3," December 3, 2003.

[252] Immigration and Refugee Protection Act, 2001 S.C., ch. 27 (Can.), at http://laws.justice.gc.ca/en/I-2.5/text.html (retrieved December 16, 2005) [Exhibit 13].

[253] "Immigration and Refugee Protection Regulations," SOR/2002-227 (Can.), at http://laws.justice.gc.ca/en/I-2.5/SOR-2002-227/text.html (retrieved December 16, 2005) [Exhibit 14].

Marriage Act,[254] which Parliament amended in 2005 to allow couples to marry regardless of gender. Through these provisions, a same-sex couple may immigrate to Canada in the same ways as opposite-sex couples.

Under Canadian law, a Canadian citizen or permanent resident may sponsor his or her partner for immigration purposes in three ways: as a *spouse*, as a *common law partner* or as a *conjugal partner*.[255]

A citizen or permanent resident can sponsor a partner (either same-sex or opposite-sex) as a *spouse* if the couple is married and standard additional criteria are met (for instance, the foreign national is sixteen or older).[256] For opposite-sex couples, a marriage that occurs outside of Canada is valid as long as it is valid both in the jurisdiction where it took place and under Canadian law.[257] However, for same-sex couples, Citizenship and Immigration Canada (CIC), the Canadian government agency in charge of immigration, has developed an "interim policy" which requires same-sex couples to marry in Canada.[258] A Canadian citizen or permanent resident who legally married his/her same-sex partner in Belgium, for example, would not appear to be able to sponsor the partner as a spouse unless they also married in Canada. This is one of the few distinctions between same-sex and opposite-sex couples under Canadian immigration law.[259]

To qualify as *common-law partners*, a couple must have cohabitated in a conjugal relationship continuously for at least one year.[260] Some of the evidence that CIC considers in determining cohabitation includes: joint bank accounts, joint ownership of home, a joint lease, and/or joint management of household expenses.[261]

---

[254] Civil Marriage Act, 2005, S.C. ch. 33, para. 2. (defining "marriage" in Canada as "the lawful union of two persons to the exclusion of all others.") at http://www.parl.gc.ca/38/1/parlbus/chambus/house/bills/government/C-38/C-38_4/C-38-3E.html (retrieved December 16, 2005).

[255] Unlike many countries, Canada allows citizens or permanent residents to sponsor partners regardless of their income level. Specifically, Canadian law exempts a sponsor from any income requirements as long as the sponsor is reasonably unencumbered by dependents and is not receiving social assistance for a reason other than disability ("Immigration and Refugee Protection Regulations," para. 133).

[256] "Immigration and Refugee Protection Regulations," para. 5.

[257] "Immigration and Refugee Protection Regulations," para. 2: "definition of 'marriage.'"

[258] CIC, "Spouse, Common-Law Partners and Conjugal Partners," pp. 1-2, at http://www.cic.gc.ca/english/sponsor/familymembers.html (retrieved December 16, 2005).

[259] Robert Hughes, "December 2004 Update on Same-Sex Marriage and Immigration," (Jan. 3, 2005), at http://www.smith-hughes.com/same-sex-marriage.html (retrieved December 16, 2005).

[260] Immigration and Refugee Regulations, para. 1; see also CIC, "Spouse, Common-Law Partners and Conjugal Partners," p. 2.

[261] CIC, "Spouse, Common-Law Partners and Conjugal Partners," p. 2.

The third way that a Canadian citizen or permanent resident can sponsor a partner (either same-sex or opposite-sex) is as a "conjugal partner." Canadian law defines a conjugal partner as a foreign national residing outside of Canada who is in a conjugal relationship (but not cohabiting) with the Canadian sponsor for a period of at least one year.[262] CIC defines a conjugal relationship as "more than a physical relationship. It is a mutually dependant relationship, and it has some permanence and the same level of commitment as a marriage or a common-law union."[263]

Two distinctions between a conjugal partner and a spouse or common-law partner are important: first, a conjugal partner must reside outside of Canada; second, CIC allows immigration under this category only when "exceptional circumstances" prevent the couple from living together. The couple must prove such an impediment, such as an immigration barrier or a marriage to someone else living in a country where divorce is not possible. The CIC expressly recognizes a same-sex relationship in a place where same-sex marriage is not permitted as a basis for claiming conjugal status.

Applicants for permanent residence as spouses or partners can generally also apply for work permits. CIC recently announced a new policy that allows both common-law partners and spouses to remain in Canada while applying for permanent residence, regardless of their immigration status.[264] For example, even if a common-law partner does not have a valid temporary immigration status, he or she may remain in Canada during the application process. However, it appears these applicants may apply for a work permit only after they receive approval in principle.[265]

Denmark

Danish nationals and permanent residents can sponsor foreign same-sex partners as part of a broader partnership recognition policy dating back to 1989, when Denmark became the first country to register lesbian and gay partnerships.[266] The same general immigration requirements apply to registered partners and married couples.

---

[262] "Immigration and Refugee Protection Regulations," para. 2.

[263] CIC, "Spouse, Common-Law Partners and Conjugal Partners," p. 3.

[264] CIC, "Change in Policy: Sponsorship of Spouses and Common-Law Partners from within Canada," at http://www.cic.gc.ca/english/sponsor/faq-spouse.html (retrieved December 16, 2005).

[265] CIC, "Change in Policy: Sponsorship of Spouses and Common-Law Partners from within Canada."

[266] The Danish Registered Partnership Act, D/341- H- ML Act No. 372 of June 1, 1989, at http://users.cybercity.dk/~dko12530/s2.htm (retrieved December 14, 2005).

In addition, a foreign partner who is neither legally registered nor married to a resident in Denmark also may apply for residence as a "cohabitating companion," so long as the couple meets the same requirements as legally recognized couples and can, in addition, demonstrate that their relationship has been a regular, long-term one (e.g., eighteen to twenty-four months at a shared address).[267]

Usually, residence permits should be applied for in the foreign partner's country of origin or domicile, but if the partner is legally in Denmark in another immigration category, he or she can apply there. Immigration requirements for spouses, registered partners and cohabitating companions include:

- That they be at least twenty-four years old;
- That the partners have a greater attachment to Denmark than to another country;
- That the partner already resident in Denmark must own or rent reasonable accommodation;
- That the partner already resident in Denmark must be able to support his/her partner.[268]

Finland

Since 2001, Finland has granted immigration benefits to same-sex couples as part of a broader partnership recognition policy.[269] The spouse (a term used whether the relationship is a marriage or registered partnership) or cohabitant (defined as living together for at least two years or having joint custody of a child) of a Finnish citizen or permanent resident may apply for a residence permit on the basis of family ties.[270] The partners' genders are irrelevant. Only spouses, cohabitants, and unmarried children

---

[267] Danish Immigration Services, "Spouses and Cohabitating Companions," http://www.udlst.dk/english/Family+Reunification/Spouses/Default.htm (retrieved December 12, 2005).

[268] Ibid; see also Aliens (Consolidation) Act No. 685 of 24 July 2003, § 9, http://www.inm.dk/imagesUpload/dokument/Aliens%20(Consolidation)%20Act%20685.pdf (retrieved December 12, 2005) (English version does not reflect recent updates to the Act).

[269] Act on Registered Partnerships, Law No. 950/2001.

[270] Aliens Act, 301/2004, § 37; Directorate of Immigration, "Perheenjäsenet," http://www.uvi.fi/netcomm/content.asp?path=8,2472,2491 (retrieved December 13, 2005).

under the age of eighteen whose guardian is living in Finland qualify as family members for immigration purposes.[271]

The spouse or cohabitant of a foreign national living in Finland must apply for a residence permit before coming to Finland and must remain abroad while waiting for a decision, unless granted a visa for a visit. However, the spouse or cohabitant of a Finnish citizen may come to Finland without getting a residence permit in advance and may stay in Finland until the application is decided.[272]

A decision on a residence application is typically reached in four to six months. The application must be supported by appropriate documentation (proof of marriage, registered partnership, or cohabitation).

France

The "Pacte Civil de Solidarité" law ("PACS," or Civil Solidarity Pact), was passed by the French National Assembly in 1999. It offers all unmarried couples, same-sex and opposite-sex, a legal status carrying some but not all of the benefits of marriage.[273] The act defines the PACS as "a contract concluded between two physical persons who have reached the age of majority, of different or the same gender, for the purposes of organizing their life in common."[274]

A foreign partner in a PACS with a French citizen can obtain a temporary residence permit ("*permit de sejour*") after a one-year waiting period. It is subject to annual renewal through the local mayor's office. After five years, a *permit de sejour* holder is eligible to apply for permanent residency (which in France means a ten-year permit).[275] Article 12 of the PACS law states that in considering the grant of permanent residency to a foreign partner, the existence of a Pact is "one of the elements for assessing personal connections in France."

---

[271] Ibid. However, for an EU citizen living in Finland, the definition of family members is broader. See Directorate of Immigration, "EU-kansalaisten perheenjäsenten oleskeluoikeus Suomessa," at http://www.uvi.fi/netcomm/content.asp?path=8,2472,2492 (retrieved December 13, 2005).

[272] Directorate of Immigration, "Oleskeluluvan hakeminen perhesiteen perusteella: Miten oleskelulupaa haetaan?" at http://www.uvi.fi/netcomm/content.asp?path=8,2472,2491,2496 (retrieved December 13, 2005).

[273] For example, couples in a PACS are taxed jointly, but only after a three-year waiting period. They cannot adopt jointly (though single-parent adoption is possible).

[274] Frédéric Martel, "The PACS—A Civil Solidarity Pact" (July 2001), at http://www.ambafrance-us.org/atoz/pacs.asp (retrieved December 14, 2005), distributed by the French Embassy in the United States.

[275] "Europe—residency requirements," U.K. Lesbian and Gay Immigration Group, at http://www.uklgig.org.uk/Europe-Residency.htm (retrieved February 7, 2006).

The Ministry of the Interior has said that a PACS has to be at least three years old to be considered a defining factor for a permanent residency application. A PACS less than three years old can still be a contributing factor, but the weight attached to it will be at the discretion of authorities in the local area (*Département*).[276]

Germany

In a 1996 decision, the Higher Administrative Court in Münster, which has sole jurisdiction in Germany over visa appeals, ruled that the European Convention on Human Rights required that the same-sex foreign partner of a German national be granted a residence permit. The government was thus obliged to give a visa to a Romanian citizen so that he could join his German partner. However, the decision was disregarded in many *Länder* (provinces), which have broad authority in Germany's federal system.[277]

The Lifetime Partnership Act, passed by the Federal Parliament, entered into force on August 1, 2001. It allowed same-sex couples throughout Germany to enter a new legal status (*Eingetragene Lebenspartnerschaft,* "registered life partnership") carrying most of the rights enjoyed by married heterosexual couples.[278]

In particular, the law opened equal immigration rights to same-sex couples. The foreign partner of a German national or resident can apply for a "long-stay visa" at a German consulate in their country, showing their partner's sponsorship and the intention of registering their partnership after arriving in Germany. Foreign partners already in Germany, as temporary residents or visitors, can change their status to permanent resident once the partnership is registered.

If the sponsor is a German citizen or permanent resident, their partner has a legal right to a residence permit. If the sponsor is a citizen of another European Union country

---

[276] Ibid.

[277] Equality for Lesbians and Gay Men: A Relevant Issue in the Civil and Social Dialogue, ILGA-Europe (the European Region of the International Lesbian and Gay Association), 1998, at http://www.ilga-europe.org/europe/publications/non_periodical/equality_for_lesbians_and_gay_men_a_relevant_issue_in_the_civil_and_political_dialogue_1998 (retrieved February 7, 2006).

[278] Russel Miler & Volker Röben, "Constitutional Court Upholds Lifetime Partnership Act," *German Law Journal*, vol. 3, no. (2002), at http://www.germanlawjournal.com/print.php?id=176 (retrieved December 7, 2005). In 2004 the Federal Parliament amended the act to increase the rights accorded registered life partnerships, but still retaining special tax and other benefits for heterosexual marriage.

working in Germany with a temporary "EU residence permit," granting residence to the partner remains discretionary. All sponsoring partners have to show:

- That he or she is financially able to support both partners;
- That he or she is not receiving social assistance.[279]

Iceland

In 1996, Iceland created the status of registered partnerships for same-sex couples.[280] Since then, Iceland has recognized immigration rights for the foreign same-sex partners of its citizens and long-term residents. Article 13 of the Act on Foreigners includes not only a person in a registered partnership but also a cohabiting partner as among the "closest family members" entitled to reside in Iceland under a "Permit to Stay."[281]

Iceland's Regulation on Foreigners codifies these immigration rights. It stipulates that both registered partners and cohabiting partners must:

- Be eighteen;
- "Be able to demonstrate that they have lived together in registered cohabitation or cohabitation otherwise confirmed for at least two years, and intend to continue their cohabitation."[282]

---

[279] "Europe--residency requirements," U.K. Lesbian and Gay Immigration Group, at http://www.uklgig.org.uk/Europe-Residency.htm (retrieved February 7, 2006).

[280] Act on Registered Partnership, No. 87 (June 12, 1996), at http://eng.domsmalaraduneyti.is/laws-and-regulations/nr/117 (retrieved December 8, 2005).

[281] Generally, people may reside in Iceland under either Permits to Stay or Residence Permits. Permits to Stay are granted first; then after one has resided in Iceland for three years and completed the required language course, one may apply for a Residence Permit, giving the right to stay indefinitely. Including of cohabiting partners in the Act is significant because registered partnerships are only open to couples where one partner is an Icelandic national; adding cohabiting partners in principle extends immigration opportunities to the foreign partners of permanent residents in Iceland. However, it is not clear whether the Icelandic term óvígð sambúð--cohabiting partner--which is usually used for opposite-sex couples, in actual legal practice covers lesbian and gay couples. See Hrefna Fridriksdóttir and Kees Waaldijk, "Major legal consequences of marriage, cohabitation and registered partnership for different-sex and same-sex partners in Iceland," in Kees Waaldijk, ed., More or Less Together: Levels of legal consequences of marriage, cohabitation and registered partnerships for different-sex and same-sex partners: A comparative study of nine European countries, Documents de travail n°125, Ined. (2005), at http://www-same-sex.ined.fr/publica_doc125.htm (retrieved February 8, 2006). See also Act on Foreigners, No. 96 (May 15, 2002), at http://eng.domsmalaraduneyti.is/laws-and-regulations/nr/105 (retrieved February 8, 2006).

[282] "Regulation on Foreigners" (No. 53 of January 23, 2003 with amendments of July 8, 2003, since amended by regulation 769/2004 of September 20, 2004), article 47, at http://eng.domsmalaraduneyti.is/laws-and-regulations/nr/860 (retrieved February 8, 2006).

The two-year requirement does not apply to married couples. In other respects, however, foreign registered partners and cohabiting partners enjoy essentially the same immigration rights as married spouses, including the right to turn a Permit to Stay into permanent residence.[283] To obtain a Permit to Stay, any foreigner must show:

- A source of financial support;
- Secure lodging;
- Adequate medical insurance.

Israel

Israel offers no national-level legal status for same-sex relationships. Nonetheless, in 2000 the Ministry of Interior moved to recognize unmarried relationships—both heterosexual and homosexual—for immigration purposes.[284] The policy has undergone several minor alterations since. In its present form,[285] the couple must satisfy ministry officials that their relationship is genuine or "sincere" and that they are running a home together; the foreign national is then granted a one-year work permit. After a year and after a re-examination, the foreign national can receive temporary resident status. This status is renewed yearly. After seven years, the foreign national can become a permanent resident.

This differs from the procedure for a foreign national in a heterosexual marriage to an Israel citizen or resident, who can receive a temporary resident visa after six months and is eligible to become for full citizenship four years later.

While married binational couples' immigration rights are specified as an entitlement in the Citizenship Law of 1952, the allowance for unmarried couples arises from the discretionary powers given the Ministry of Interior in the Law of Entry into Israel of 1952. As a result, courts have been reluctant to override the Ministry's judgment in particular cases. Activists have complained that the Ministry has never put forward

---

[283] A foreigner married to an opposite-sex Icelandic national with whom the foreigner has lived in Iceland for three years does not need a Permit to Stay; this exemption is not available for registered or cohabiting partners.

[284] For a detailed overall discussion of the issue, see Oded Feller, Attorney, Association for Civil Rights Israel (ACRI), "The Immigration Rights of Same-Sex Couples," at http://www.acri. org.il/english-acri/engine/story.asp?id=256 (retrieved January 24, 2006).

[285] Population Registry regulation 5.2.0009, at http://www.moin.gov.il/Apps/PubWebSite/publications.nsf/All/9CD5C9CFC6C82B85422570AD00431263/$FILE/Publications.2.0009.pdf?OpenElement (retrieved January 26, 2006).

criteria for the "sincerity" of an unmarried relationship, whether opposite-sex or same-sex, leaving the decision to the whims of individual officials. A case now before the Supreme Court would require the Ministry to stipulate what evidence a couple must present to prove their relationship is genuine.[286]

Netherlands

Dutch law, much like Canada's, extends broad and equal immigration rights to same-sex binational couples.[287] Same-sex and opposite-sex couples have the same three options for legal recognition of their relationship: civil marriage, registered partnership, or a cohabitation agreement.[288]

Under Dutch law, the foreign spouse, registered partner, or unmarried or unregistered partner of a resident of the Netherlands is entitled to a Provisional Residence Permit, as the first step toward a full residence permit. The application can be made in the Netherlands or at a consulate abroad. The couple must show that they:

- Intend to live together in a joint household in the Netherlands;
- Are both at least eighteen;
- Are both unmarried to anyone else.

The Dutch resident sponsor:

- Must have a long-term job;

[286] Appeal in Administrative Petition 9273/05, *Louis Gonzalez Garcia v The Minister of the Interior.* In a separate case, the Supreme Court will also hear a complaint against the Ministry's requirement that an unmarried foreign-national spouse, if in Israel illegally, must leave the country during processing of the residency application—a condition not imposed on married spouses: Appeal in Administrative Petition 4614/05 *The State of Israel – The Ministry of the Interior v Avner Oren*.

[287] For Dutch immigration law information published in English by the Ministerie van Justice, Immigratie, nen Naturalisatiedienst, see generally http://www.ind.nl/EN/algemeen/ brochures/Downloaden/index.asp?subhome=&title=&origin=. An overall guide can be found in Kees Waaldijk, "Major legal consequences of marriage, cohabitation and registered partnership for different-sex and same-sex partners in the Netherlands," in Kees Waaldijk, ed., *More or Less Together: Levels of legal consequences of marriage, cohabitation and registered partnerships for different-sex and same-sex partners: A comparative study of nine European countries*, Documents de travail n°125, Ined. (2005), at http://www-same-sex.ined.fr/publica_doc125.htm (retrieved February 8, 2006).

[288] "Marriage, Registered Partnership and Cohabitation," brochure published by the Dutch Ministry of Justice: http://www.justitie.nl/english/Images/marriage_ registered_tcm75-28560.pdf (retrieved December 20, 2005).

- Must earn at least the family minimum wage set by the National Assistance Act.[289]

For two foreigners to marry or form a registered partnership (either same-sex or opposite-sex), one of them must either have a permanent residence permit or obtain a statement from the Aliens Police specifying his or her status under the Aliens Act.[290] Thus, under Dutch law, it is unlikely that two foreigners could immigrate together to the Netherlands as a couple unless one of them already legally lived there.[291]

New Zealand

New Zealand allows eligible citizens and residents to sponsor a foreign partner's residency application. The 1999 Immigration Regulations define "partner" as "the civil union partner or *de facto* partner of the applicant." [292] (In 2004, Parliament voted to create the status of civil unions for both same-sex and opposite-sex couples, giving the same rights as marriage under a different name.) Evidence of the partnership can include:

- A marriage or civil union certificate;
- Evidence of exclusivity and emotional commitment, such as joint decision-making, sharing of household duties, or parental responsibilities;
- Financial dependence or interdependence, such as shared income, bank accounts, money transfers to and from one another's accounts;
- Evidence of communication if significant time was spent apart;

---

[289] "Europe--residency requirements," U.K. Lesbian and Gay Immigration Group, at http://www.uklgig.org.uk/Europe-Residency.htm (retrieved February 7, 2006). See also *More or Less Together*, p. 146: "articles 3.13 to 3.17 of the Aliens Decree 2000 (*Vreemdelingenbesluit 2000, Staatsblad 497,* in force since April 1, 2001) allow for the immigration of married, registered and unmarried/unregistered partners, provided that they live together and have a joint household. One of the conditions is that the 'receiving' partner has a sufficient income, *i.e.* 100% of the official minimum wage ... Until April 1, 2001 the right to immigration of partners was contained in policy guidelines (*Vreemdelingencirculaire*), which since 1975 recognized informally cohabiting different-sex and same-sex partners of Dutch citizens." See also A.H.J. Swart, *De toelating en uitzetting van vreemdelingen*, (Deventer: Kluwer, 1978), pp. 165-166, and "Marriage, Registered Partnership and Cohabitation," p. 4.

[290] "Marriage, Registered Partnership and Cohabitation," pp. 4-5.

[291] See also "Residence in the Netherlands: Appendix 3: Staying with a family member," p. 18 (November 2004), available in English from the Ministerie van Justice, Immigratie - en Naturalisatiedienst at http://www.ind.nl/en/Images/Verblijf_ENG_tcm6-595.pdf (retrieved February 8, 2006).

[292] Immigration Regulations 1999, regulation 20 ("Applications Involving Family Members"), at http://www.legislation.govt.nz/browse_vw.asp?content-set=pal_regs (retrieved December 14, 2005).

- Evidence of the duration of the relationship;
- Photographs together, or evidence of public or family recognition of the relationship;
- Proof of shared residence.

To apply, the couple must:

- Be living together for at least one year in a genuine and committed relationship;
- Be eighteen or over, or between sixteen and eighteen if they have the legal consent of parents or guardians;
- Have met before the residence application was made;
- Not be relatives.[293]

Immigration authorities must be satisfied that the relationship is "genuine and stable" and that the partners intend "to remain in it long-term and to be exclusive to each other [and] that the relationship is likely to last."[294]

The couple can live together in New Zealand while awaiting a residence visa, and officials may give the immigrating partner a work visa or work permit before issuing the residence visa, so that the couple can fulfill the twelve-month cohabitation requirement,.[295]

---

[293] Additional requirements are that the applicant be "of good health" and "good character." The Immigration Service states that "Generally, we will not approve people for residence in New Zealand if they: require dialysis treatment; have active pulmonary tuberculosis (TB); have severe haemophilia; have a physical incapacity that requires full time care." It will also decline applicants if "likely to impose significant costs or demands on New Zealand's health services or special education services." HIV/AIDS is often taken to indicate this. "Good character" entails excluding serious criminal offenses. See New Zealand Immigration Service, "Can I Move to New Zealand?" at http://www.immigration.govt.nz/migrant/stream/live/partner/canimovetonz/whatisrequired/ (retrieved February 8, 2006).

[294] New Zealand Immigration Service, "Requirements," http://www.immigration.govt.nz/migrant/stream/live/partner/canimovetonz/whatisrequired/ and "Summary of Terms", http://glossaryImmigration.govt.nz/Genuineandstablerelationship.htm (retrieved December 14, 2005).

[295] New Zealand Immigration Service, "Residence," at 69-11 (December 21, 2005), at http://www.immigration.govt.nz/NR/rdonlyres/B9297CAD-5D25-43BE-AFBC-FACA87C79884/0/Residence.pdf (retrieved January 10, 2006), and New Zealand Department of Labour's Form NZIS 1015 which is used to obtain a permit for those who do not have permanent residence rights in New Zealand, at http://www.immigration.govt.nz/NR/rdonlyres/EC9A6BEF-1152-482F-B39F-B782EE7688FA/0/1015June24.pdf (retrieved January 26, 2006).

An eligible sponsor must be a citizen or resident of New Zealand and must not have been "the perpetrator of an incident of domestic violence which resulted in the grant of permanent residence to a person under [the asylum] policy for victims of domestic violence."[296] If that citizen partner has already sponsored someone for immigration, they cannot sponsor another person for five years.

Once granted a residence visa, the foreign partner can then apply for a residence permit, which allows him or her to live, work, and study in New Zealand indefinitely.

Norway

In 1993, through the Registered Partnership Act, Norway provided legal recognition to same-sex couples.[297] A registered partnership has most of the legal rights of a heterosexual marriage.[298] Provisions of Norwegian legislation dealing with marriage and spouses apply equally to registered partners.

The foreign spouse or registered partner of a Norwegian citizen need merely prove that the citizen partner lives or intends to live in Norway. The foreign partner of a non-Norwegian national who has Norwegian residency must also prove that the two have been married or in a registered partnership for at least three years.[299] Additional requirements include that both partners were over eighteen when they entered into the marriage/partnership and that the sponsoring spouse/partner show sufficient income to support them. [300]

Immigration rights are also available to foreign unmarried and unregistered "cohabitating partners" of Norwegian citizens or residents. They must show that they have "lived together in a permanent and established relationship as cohabitants for at least two years

---

[296] New Zealand Immigration Service, "Eligible Sponsor," http://www.immigration.govt.nz/migrant/stream/live/partner/canisponsormypartner/eligiblesponsor.htm (retrieved December 14, 2005).

[297] Registered Partnership Act No. 40 (April 30, 1993), at http://odin.dep.no/bfd/english/doc/ handbooks/004041-120003/dok-bn.html (retrieved December 20, 2005).

[298] Despite strengthening of the law in 2000 and 2001, inequalities in adoption and parenting rights remain. In 2004, Norway's parliament rejected a bill that would have instituted full equality in civil marriage.

[299] *Utlendingsdirektoratet* (UDI, Norwegian Directorate of Immigration) Circular 2003-015, "Visa For Foreign Spouse, Joint Child(ren) or Registered Same-Sex Marriage Partner Applying for Family Reunification," p.2 (June 5, 2003), at http://www.udi.no/templates/Rundskriv.aspx?id=5005 (retrieved February 8, 2006).

[300] UDI Circular 2003-015, p. 2, states that the "subsistence requirement" equals the pay grade for civil service employees grade 1: UDI Fact Sheet, "Family immigration," (Aug. 29, 2005) states that the "subsistence requirement" as of March 1, 2005 equaled NOK 169,100 annually before taxes—approximately $25,000 US; at http://www.udi.no/upload/Faktaark/Engelsk/Familiegjenforening_engelsk.pdf (retrieved December 17, 2005).

and intend to continue their cohabitation." Exceptions are possible where, "because of work or other practical reasons," they have been unable to live together; partners can "document contact on a regular basis" along with "concrete plans to move together to a joint residence." [301]

The Registered Partnership Act limits two foreign nationals' ability to enter into a registered partnership with each other. For example, at least one of the parties must have been a resident of Norway for two years prior to registration.[302] While both foreign nationals must be "lawfully resident" in the country, [303] this can include residence on temporary or visitors' visas.[304]

Portugal

In 2001, Portugal's Parliament passed a "Law on the Protection of *De Facto* Unions," which extended the legal status of *de facto* couples, or common-law spouses, to any couple "independent of sex" who could show that they had cohabited for more than two years. The benefits accorded such couples were substantially less than those of heterosexual marriage but included inheritance, pension, insurance and tax rights.[305]

The government recognized these relationships for immigration purposes by extending "authorization for residence" to same-sex partners in a *de facto* union with Portuguese citizens or permanent residents.[306] Applicants must provide:

- Proof of unmarried status;
- Other documents proving common-law partnership for at least two years," including "joint bank accounts, joint individual tax return and other relevant means of proof";

---

[301] UDI Circular 89/2002, "Section 23 first paragraph (b): The requirement of a permanent and established relationship as cohabitants," at http://www.udi.no/templates/Rundskriv.aspx?id=4600 (retrieved February 8, 2006).

[302] Registered Partnership Act, Section 2.

[303] See Ministry of Children and Family Affairs Brochure, "Registered Partnership," ap.3 (No. Q-0832 E), at http://odin.dep.no/bfd/english/doc/handbooks/004041-120003/dok-bn.html (retrieved December 14, 2005).

[304] Ibid.

[305] Lei Nº 7/2001 de 11 de Maio, Adopta medidas de protecção das uniões de facto, at http://portugalgay.pt/politica/parlamento03.asp (retrieved February 8, 2006).

[306] Decree-Law No, 34/2003 of 25 February 25, 2003, "Approving the conditions for the entry, permanence, exit and removal of foreign nationals from Portugal," article 87, at the website of the *Serviço de Estrangeiros e Fronteiras* (SEF), http://www.sef.pt/legislacao.uk.php (retrieved February 8, 2006).

- Proof of accommodation in Portugal;
- Proof of means of subsistence in Portugal;
- Any criminal records.[307]

At first, the partner will receive a temporary authorization for residence, valid for two years and renewable for successive periods of three years. After either five years (for citizens of lusophone countries) or eight years (for other nationals), the partner is eligible for a permanent residence authorization.[308]

In 2004, Portugal amended its constitution to include "sexual orientation" as a status protected against discrimination.

South Africa

On December 2, 1999, South Africa's Constitutional Court held that a foreign partner in a same-sex relationship with a citizen or permanent resident must be afforded the same immigration rights as a married person. Relying on sweeping constitutional protections, the court held that denying those rights discriminated unfairly against lesbians and gays on the grounds of sexual orientation and marital status and seriously limited their equality rights and their right to dignity.[309]

The decision took effect immediately and with little fanfare, but Parliament later amended the immigration laws. The Immigration Act of 2002 provided that "the Department [of Home Affairs] shall issue a permanent residence permit to a foreigner who…is the spouse of a citizen or resident." It defined "spouse" as "a person who is party to a marriage, or a customary union, or to a permanent homosexual or heterosexual relationship which calls for cohabitation and mutual financial and emotional support, and is proven by a prescribed affidavit substantiated by a notarial

---

307 SEF, "Foreign citizens living in a common law partnership with a Portuguese citizen or legal resident, as laid down by law," at
http://www.sef.pt/ajuda.uk.php (retrieved February 8, 2006).

308 SEF, "Types of Authorisation for Residence," at http://www.sef.pt/ajuda.uk.php (retrieved February 8, 2006).

309 *National Coalition for Gay and Lesbian Equality and Others v. The Minister of Home Affairs and Others*, Constitutional Court of South Africa, CCT 10/99 at 97.

contract."[310] Provisions in the Immigration Act of (?) 2002 about obtaining permits for employment[311] also extended equally to same-sex partners.

In 2005, the Constitutional Court decided that the full title and rights of marriage enjoyed by heterosexual couples could not be denied to lesbian and gay couples.[312] It gave Parliament one year to amend legislation accordingly. Since same-sex partners already enjoyed parity with opposite-sex couples under South African immigration law, the decision did not extend their immigration rights.

Spain

An amendment to the Civil Marriage Code in Spain to allow equality in civil marriage for same-sex couples took effect on July 3, 2005.[313]

Implementation of the amended Code is in its earliest stages. Only days after it became law, officials in Catalonia denied a marriage license to a Spanish national and his Indian partner on the grounds that India did not permit same-sex marriage.[314] However, on July 27, 2005, the *Junta de Fiscales de Sala*, a body of attorneys advising the *Fiscal General del Estado* (the national attorney general's office), handed down an official opinion, published in the state bulletin, that the right of Spanish nationals to marry foreign same-sex partners could not depend on foreign legislation. The opinion held that "a marriage between a Spaniard and a foreigner, or between foreigners of the same sex resident in Spain, shall be valid as a result of applying Spanish material law, even if the foreigner's national legislation does not allow or recognize the validity of such marriages."[315]

---

[310] Immigration Act, 2002, Act. No. 13, 2002, as published in the Government Gazette, vol. 443, no. 23478 (May 31, 2002), Section 1 (xxxvi) at 12.

[311] Ibid., Section 27(a)(iv) at 42.

[312] *Minister of Home Affairs and Others v Fourie and Bonthuys and Others*, Constitutional Court of South Africa, CCT 60/04.

[313] Ley 13/2005, de 1 de julio, por la que se modifica el Código Civil en materia de derecho a contraer matrimonio, at http://www.boe.es/boe/dias/2005/07/02/pdfs/ A23632-23634.pdf (retrieved December 18, 2005).

[314] Daniel Woolls, "Spain's Gay Marriage Law Hits Snag Over Foreigners," Associated Press*,* July 6, 2005.

[315] See "Spain's same-sex marriage law applies to foreigners," Associated Press, July 27, 2005, and "Fiscalía acuerda apoyar los matrimonios gays entre españoles y extranjeros," Europa Press, July 27, 2005.

Sweden

Sweden provides immigration rights to binational same-sex couples as part of a broader policy recognizing same-sex relationships. Sweden created the category of registered partnerships for such relationships in 1994.[316] In addition, in 2003 a gender-neutral act on cohabitation gave same-sex cohabiting couples who have not entered a registered partnership the same rights and responsibilities as their unmarried opposite-sex counterparts. A foreigner may obtain a residence permit on the basis of family ties if he or she is or plans to be *married* to, entering a *registered partnership* with, or *cohabiting* with a Swedish national or resident.[317] Partners in same-sex or opposite-sex relationships are subject to the same immigration requirements.

The partner seeking a residence permit must normally apply to a Swedish consulate in their country of residence. The consulate will interview the applicant and review documentation—letters, photographs, a marriage or registered-partnership certificate, or evidence of cohabitation—proving the relationship to the person in Sweden. The consulate then will forward the application to the Migration Board in Sweden.[318]

Residence permits are normally granted on a yearly basis for the first two years. After that, if the Migration Board decides the relationship is still a serious one, the foreign partner can be granted a permanent residence permit. If the partners—whether married, registered, or cohabiting—have lived together for at least two years before the move to Sweden, the foreign partner may receive a permanent residence permit immediately.[319]

Switzerland

In 2003, after two cantons (Geneva and Zurich) had passed bills giving registered-partners status to lesbian and gay couples, the Swiss federal government began opening

---

[316] Registered Partnership Act, Law 1994/1117, at http://www.france.qrd.org/texts/partnership/se/sweden-act.html (retrieved December 7, 2005).

[317] Swedish Migration Board, "Swedish Residence Permits by Reason of Family Ties," at http://www.migrationsverket.se/english.jsp (retrieved December 16, 2005); see also the Alien Act (Utlänningslagen), Law 1989/529, at http://www.immi.se/lagar/1989529.htm (retrieved December 16, 2005).

[318] "Swedish Residence Permits by Reason of Family Ties."

[319] "Europe--residency requirements," U.K. Lesbian and Gay Immigration Group, at http://www.uklgig.org.uk/Europe-Residency.htm (retrieved February 7, 2006).

immigration rights to foreign same-sex partners of Swiss nationals and residents, provided they could prove a stable and committed relationship of at least one year.[320]

However, in 2004, the federal parliament passed a bill creating registered partnerships for same-sex couples at the national level. This status gave most of the rights of marriage to those partners, excepting adoption and access to reproductive technologies. The bill amended immigration law to extend the same rights to registered partners as to heterosexual spouses and mandated that marriages and civil partnerships between people of the same sex validly entered into in other countries would be recognized in Switzerland.[321]

Opponents forced a national referendum on the law; on June 5, 2005, voters approved it with a 58% majority. It will take effect in 2007.

A Swiss national or resident's foreign same-sex partner, if living outside the country, will be able to apply for a three-month visa to visit Switzerland and conclude a registered partnership. After the partnership is registered, the foreign partner is eligible for a Type B residence permit, which allows work and provides exemption from all labor market restrictions applying to foreign nationals. It is annually renewable provided the partnership is not dissolved, and can be converted into a Type C permanent residence permit after five years.

United Kingdom

The United Kingdom began providing limited immigration rights to binational lesbian and gay couples in 1997, when the government announced the "Concession Outside the Immigration Rules for Unmarried Partners."[322] (A concession is a policy decision which, while not written in the Immigration Rules, must be implemented by immigration officers.) The Unmarried Partners Concession made it possible for U.K. residents to

---

[320] Yves de Matteis, "Couples Binationaux: La Directive qui Change Tout," *360° Magazine*, July-August 2003, at http://www.360.ch/presse/2003/07/couples_binationaux_la_directive_qui_change_tout.php (retrieved February 8, 2006).

[321] Loi fédérale sur le partenariat enregistré entre personnes du même sexe

(Loi sur le partenariat; LPart) du 18 juin 2004, at http://www.admin.ch/ch/f/ff/2004/2935.pdf (retrieved February 8, 2006).

[322] Information on the Unmarried Partners Concession is available on the website of the U.K. Lesbian & Gay Immigration Group at http://www.uklgig.org.uk/docs/UKLGIG%20Information.doc (retrieved January 10, 2006). See also Chris Duenas, "Coming to America: The Immigration Obstacle Facing Binational Same-Sex Couples," *Southern California Law Review,* vol. 73 (2000), pp. 811–841.

apply for their foreign same-sex partner to enter the country—*if* they had already lived together for four years. This requirement posed a heavy burden. The Home Minister himself admitted that the criteria were "strict—and much tighter than for those who can marry."[323] In 1999, the required cohabitation period was reduced to two years. In October 2000, the Unmarried Partners Concession was made into an Immigration Rule, giving it statutory force.[324]

On December 5, 2005, the inequality ended when the Civil Partnership Act ("CPA") became U.K. law. It legally recognizes same-sex couples in a committed relationship—and provides binational same-sex couples with immigration rights equal to those enjoyed by opposite-sex couples. Immigration laws were amended to include references to civil partnerships wherever spouses were mentioned.[325]

A civil partnership can be formed by two people of the same sex, over sixteen years old, who are not already in such a partnership with, or married to, others. It can be created in the U.K. through a registration ceremony, but comparable relationships formalized in other countries (not just at the federal level in countries such as Sweden or South Africa, but in states such as California or Vermont) can also be recognized as civil partnerships.[326]

The foreign civil partner of a British national or permanent resident is thus eligible for U.K. immigration on the same terms as a heterosexual spouse. An entry clearance for a "proposed civil partner" (similar to a fiancé/e) allows him or her to come to the U.K. in order to register the partnership, before switching into the "civil partner" immigration category. Such couples are not required to have resided together, but entry clearance

---

[323] Quoted in Duenas, "Coming to America."

[324] The Concession is codified in §§ 295D to 295F of the Immigration Rules, at http://www.ind.homeoffice.gov.uk/ind/en/home/laws___policy/immigration_rules/part_8/part_9.html (retrieved Jan. 10, 2006).

[325] The Immigration Rules were amended to include after each reference to a "spouse" the term "or civil partner"; after each reference to "marriage" the term "or civil partnership"; and after each reference to "fiancé(e)" the term "or proposed civil partner." Also included, analogous to the term "unmarried partner," is the term "same-sex partner." The relevant Immigration Rules are at http://www.ind.homeoffice.gov.uk/ind/en/home/laws_policy/ immigration_rules/part_8/part_9.html (retrieved December 14, 2005).

[326] The Home Office provides a non-exhaustive list of acceptable jurisdictions at http://www.ind.homeoffice.gov.uk/ind/en/home/laws___policy/policy_instructions/nis/c-d/civil_partnership.Maincontent.0002.file.tmp/Vol%202%20Sec%202.C.pdf.

officers must be satisfied that the relationship is genuine and ongoing, and that the foreign national will not have recourse to public funds before or after the ceremony.[327]

After registering the civil partnership, the applicant partner will be granted residence for up to two years.[328] After that, if the partnership continues, he or she can apply for Indefinite Leave to Remain (permanent residence).[329] Finally, civil partners of people who have temporary leave in the U.K., such as foreign students and work permit holders, can apply for permanent residence along with their civil partners.[330]

---

[327] Immigration Rules § 281(b); see also "A Guide to Civil Partnerships," U.K. Lesbian and Gay Immigration Group, at http://www.uklgig.org.uk/Civil%20Partnership.htm.

[328] Immigration Rules § 282.

[329] Ibid., §287(a)(i)(a).

[330] The Unmarried Partners Rule (formerly Concession), requiring two years' prior cohabitation, remains in force, providing an alternative if arduous route for couples who do not wish to register as civil partners.

Appendix C: Census Information on Binational Same-Sex Couples in the United States

There is currently no available data on the number of lesbian and gay immigrants and non-immigrants inside the United States; the Department of Homeland Security does not track this information. Because the United States does not recognize same-sex partnerships for immigration benefits, there are no official numbers of potential applicants who, if permitted, would apply for such status.

However, the U.S. Census reveals some relevant figures.

The 2000 census showed 594,391 couples living together who identified themselves as of the same-sex in the United States. Six percent of these, or an estimated 35,820 couples, are in binational relationships—in other words, one or both of the partners in these couples is not a U.S. citizen. This appendix provides a brief demographic portrait of binational same-sex "unmarried partners" from Census 2000.[331] In order to determine the validity and significance of these findings, it is important to understand what exactly constitutes a same-sex household.

In 1990, the census provided a way for same-sex cohabitating couples to self-identify for the first time. The census questionnaire does not specifically ask respondents about their sexual orientation, but it allows householders to identify who lives in their home and their relationship to the householder. The forms provide a range of categories for how individuals in a household are connected. These fall into two broad types: *related* persons (including husband/wife, son/daughter, brother/sister, etc.) and *unrelated* persons (including unmarried partner, housemate/roommate, roomer/border, and other non-relative). "Unmarried partner" was added to the census in 1990, partly to account for the millions of American adults—gay, straight, or bisexual—who are living together outside a state-recognized marriage. The forms define an unmarried partner as "an adult who is unrelated to the householder, but shares living quarters and has a close personal relationship with the householder." It is reasonable to assume that two people of the same sex who identify as "unmarried partners" in the census are a lesbian or gay couple.

---

[331] Data from Census 2000 are drawn from the 5% Public Use Microdata Sample (PUMS), a random sample of responses from households that received a census long-form with sample sizes equivalent to 5% of all U.S. households. The PUMS provide detailed demographic and economic information for each household sampled and analyses can be generalized to the U.S. population.

It is impossible to decipher the number of transgender and bisexual people who are found in both same-sex and different-sex relationships as defined by the census. In all likelihood, many couples counted in both categories have transgender- or bisexual-identified partners. Because of the imprecision of these terms in the census and for convenience, we will refer to the couples in this count as lesbian or gay couples.

This figure is an undercount. There are several reasons.

- The census does not allow same-sex couples who do *not* live together to report their relationship status.
- Some couples may feel that the terminology of "unmarried partner" (or "husband/wife") does not accurately describe their relationship.
- Some lesbians and gay men may not feel comfortable declaring their sexual orientation to a government agency and may have indicated a status that would not reveal the true nature of their relationship.
- The census offers categories of citizen or non-citizen but does not count lawful permanent residents (LPRs)—some of whom may also face separation if they are partnered with non-immigrants who do not have the same right to stay in the U.S.
- Finally, and perhaps most importantly, concerns about confidentiality—particularly with regard to their immigration status—may have led many foreign-born non-citizens to not report themselves or to identify as naturalized citizens on their census form.

Nor, of course, do the census figures reflect those couples who have chosen or been forced to live abroad because they cannot legally reside together in the U.S. For all these reasons, these numbers should be taken as one part of a larger whole.

Demographic Patterns

Numbers should not matter in determining the rights to which one is entitled. Politically, though, they carry weight. While not definitive, these figures suggest both the scope of the problem immigration inequality creates, and the likely impact of a legal solution.

71,640 lesbians and gay men living in the U.S. are in a relationship where one partner is a non-citizen—as stated, six percent of all same-sex couples counted as binational. By comparison, less than five percent of different-sex partners, both married and unmarried—or approximately 2,790,607 couples—are in binational couples.

Of the total number of same-sex couples captured by the census, a further 27,546 same-sex couples, or 55,092 individuals, are comprised of two non-citizens. When combined with the number of binational same-sex couples, there are 63,366 couples—126,732 lesbian and gay men, or nearly eleven percent of the same-sex couples accounted for in Census 2000—who have had to address immigration issues as part of their experience and are potentially injured by the discrimination in immigration law against lesbians and gay men.

Sex

Of the 35,820 same-sex unmarried partners identified as binational couples, 20,826 are male-male couples, or approximately 58 percent and 14,994 are female-female, or nearly 42 percent,. The proportion reflects the larger trend that the majority of foreign-born individuals within the U.S. are men.

Age

The study shows no significant difference in average age between same-sex binational couples and different-sex binational couples. In same-sex binational partnerships between two men,

- The citizen partner averages 40.4 years old;
- The non-citizen partner averages 38 years old.

Among such partnerships between two women,

- The citizen partner averages 38.9 years old;
- The non-citizen partner averages 38.7 years old.

These figures suggest a population largely of working age, actively participating in the U.S. economy through their purchasing power or tax payments or both. They also portray people concerned about aging, not only for themselves, but also for their loved ones. At forty, many American partners have built lives around extended family, friends, and often children. The choice or necessity of moving abroad will affect those lives and their communities—including people they may care for, such as aging parents.

Children in the Home

According to the Census 2000, nearly 16,000 binational same-sex couples—46 percent of the whole—are raising children, biological and non-biological, in the home. Male couples are less likely than female couples to have children, though nearly 7,300 gay male binational couples, or more than a third, report a child under eighteen living in their home. When compared with the broader population of male same-sex couples, approximately one in five of whom have children, the proportion of binational partners caring for children is substantially higher.

Same-sex female binational couples are more likely to be raising children than their different-sex unmarried counterparts, 58 percent versus 51 percent respectively.

Children under eighteen being raised by same-sex binational couples are less likely to be citizens than children being raised by different-sex binational couples. Among children of same-sex male binational partners, 83 percent are citizens, compared to 87 percent of the children of same-sex female binational partners. The comparable figures for different-sex couples are 94 percent for children being raised by unmarried couples and 90 percent for children in married couple households. A significant number of children are likely to be affected by the lack of legal recognition for the parents' relationship.

Income and Education

U.S. citizen men who are partners in same-sex binational relationships showed higher education levels than their married male equivalents—34 percent report earned a college degree as opposed to 28 percent among married male citizens. By comparison, twenty-nine percent of non-citizen men in same-sex relationships hold college degrees, a rate less than U.S. citizen men in same-sex relationships but almost equal to that of married male citizens. Education differences between citizen women in binational relationships and marriages are not as pronounced: twenty-four percent of women citizens in same-sex binational couples hold a college degree, which is almost equal to the twenty-three percent rate of college degrees among married women. There is a slightly more pronounced difference in comparison with compared with non-citizen women in same-sex binational relationships, only 20 percent of whom hold college degrees.

Male citizens in same-sex binational couples show an average income of $40,359. This is not significantly different from the figure of married male citizens, whose average income is $40,831. By comparison, there is a significant income difference between both kinds of citizen men and non-citizen men in same-sex relationships, who earn $31,781 or nearly $9,000 less.

Despite the similarities in educational background and age, men in same-sex binational couples claim substantially higher incomes than women in such couples. On average, both the citizen and non-citizen partner in female same-sex binational couples report comparable earnings slightly above $28,000 ($28,488 and $28,978 respectively). Among non-citizens, women in same-sex binational couples have average earnings nearly $3,000 higher than unmarried women partnered with men and $9,000 greater than married women. In general, citizen partners of binational couples tend to have higher incomes than their non-citizen partner/spouse. However, same-sex female couples are the exception to this pattern as non-citizen partners report a slightly greater income.

Non-citizen men who are in same-sex relationships report a low level of participation in the labor force—74 percent, compared to 81 percent of non-citizen men in different-sex unmarried couples and 80 percent of married men. Non-citizen women in binational same-sex relationships, or in different-sex unmarried partnerships, have substantially higher labor force participation rates—68 percent and 69 percent respectively—than married women, at 51 percent.

Similarly, non-citizen males in same-sex binational couples have low levels of full-time employment—only 66 percent, as opposed to more than 80 percent of non-citizen men in other binational couple types. In contrast, foreign-born women in same-sex binational couples have high levels of full-time employment at 61 percent, the same rate as non-citizen women in different-sex unmarried couples and significantly higher than their married counterparts with 41 percent employed full-time.

Military Service

Despite the strong disincentives in the current "Don't Ask, Don't Tell" policy, many lesbian and gay people continue to serve in the U.S. military. This holds true for both citizens and non-citizens. Among all same-sex binational couples, 7 percent of citizen partners report being veterans—and more than 3 percent of non-citizen partners.

Length of Residence and Relationship

The proportion of couples who report living together in the same home five years before provides some indication of relationships' stability. Same-sex binational couples are more likely (28 percent of male couples and 30 percent of female couples) than their different-sex unmarried counterparts (17 percent) to have been together at least five years. But, they less likely than their heterosexual married counterparts (41 percent) to be in the same home five years before.

Appendix D: Organizations that Work with LGBT Immigrants, Asylum Seekers, and Binational Couples

Immigration Equality

350 West 31st Street, Suite 505

New York, NY 10001

Tel. +1 (212) 714-2904

Fax +1 (212) 714-2973

E-mail: info@immigrationequality.org

www.immigrationequality.org

Immigration Equality (founded in 1994 as the Lesbian and Gay Immigration Rights Task Force) is a national organization which advocates for equality under immigration law for lesbian, gay, bisexual, transgender, (LGBT) and HIV-positive people. ImEq gives LGBT foreign nationals and their loved ones up-to-date information about immigration law through trainings, informational materials, and by answering email and telephone inquiries. ImEq runs a pro bono asylum project to assist LGBT and HIV-positive asylum seekers to find free or low-cost legal representation. Immigration Equality also maintains a list of LGBT/HIV-friendly private immigration attorneys to provide legal representation to people in need of it.

Love Sees No Borders

P.O. Box 60486

Sunnyvale, CA 94088, USA

Fax: 413- 502-4758

E-mail: info@loveseesnoborders.org

www.loveseesnoborders.org

Love Sees No Borders was established by Marta Donayre and Leslie Bulbuk in August 2001 to advocate on behalf of binational same-sex couples trying to live in the United States. Love Sees No Borders concentrates on helping couples share their stories with one another and with a broader audience, and on explaining the dynamics of same-sex immigration issues and the hardship that same-sex couples undergo because they are denied immigration rights.

The Love Exiles Foundation

Phone +31 (0)20 679 0523

E-mail: loveexiles@xs4all.nl

www.loveexiles.org

The Love Exiles Foundation supports LGBT couples who have chosen or are considering exile in order to be together. Many same-sex couples choose to immigrate to a country that recognizes their relationship for immigration purposes. They face the challenges of leaving behind their homes, communities, families, jobs and careers to start a new life. Love Exiles supports these families and educates the public about the issues same-sex couples face. There are local Love Exiles groups in Germany (Köln), the Netherlands (Amsterdam), the U.K. (London), Canada and Australia.

Asylum Documentation Program
International Gay and Lesbian Human Rights Commission

P.O. Box 558, San Francisco, CA 94104, USA
Phone: 1-415-398-2759
Fax: 1-415-398-4635
E-mail: asylum@iglhrc.org

www.iglhrc.org

The Asylum Documentation Program of the International Gay and Lesbian Human Rights Commission (IGLHRC) supports those seeking asylum or other hardship-based immigration status due to persecution based on sexual orientation, gender identity, or HIV/AIDS status. The Asylum Documentation Program supports exclusively by providing asylum-relevant country condition documentation in the form of country packets.

Immigration Project

National Center for Lesbian Rights

870 Market Street, Suite 370
San Francisco, CA 94102
Tel. + 1 (415) 392 - 6257 ext.304
Fax + 1 (415) 392 - 8442

Email: ncalonje@nclrights.org

http://www.nclrights.org

Since 1977, the National Center for Lesbian Rights has worked to create a world in which every lesbian can live fully, free from discrimination. NCLR works toward this through impact litigation, public policy advocacy, public education, direct legal services, and collaboration with other social justice organizations and activists. As part of this work, NCLR is committed to helping overcome the immigration hurdles faced by same-sex binational couples, as well as lesbian, gay, bisexual and transgender immigrants. The NCLR Immigration Project provides legal representation, support, assistance and community education to LGBT immigrants, and advocates for equitable immigration and asylum laws and policies.

Queer Immigrant Rights Project

New York, NY

For assistance and referrals regarding an immigration issue or general questions about Queer Immigrant Rights Project, please contact Ruso Panduro at rpanduro@quir.org.

Led by and comprised of LGBT and HIV+ asylees, asylum seekers and immigrants from more than 50 countries, the Queer Immigrant Rights Project aims to address issues surrounding LGBT immigrants who face isolation within their own immigrant communities and xenophobia and racism within both the queer and straight communities. The QuIR Project strives to provide a much needed "safe space" for LGBT and HIV+ immigrants to allow them to network, assist one another, share information and resources, and advocate on issues affecting the queer immigrant community.